BLASTED HEAVENS

Blasted Heavens:

Five Contemporary Plays Inspired by the Greeks

Antigone Arkhe
Lucinda Caval
Steal Back Light from the Virtual
The Tropic of X
Wreckage

By

CARIDAD SVICH

EYECORNER PRESS

© Caridad Svich & EyeCorner Press | 2012

Blasted Heavens:
Five Contemporary Plays Inspired by the Greeks

Published by EYECORNER PRESS
Roskilde, September 2012

ISBN: 978-87-92633-18-7

Cover design and layout: Camelia Elias
Cover image: Eric Kerr and Detroit Dunwood in Caridad Svich's WRECKAGE premiere at Crowded Fire Theatre Company, San Francisco, CA (2009). Photo courtesy of Crowded Fire Theatre.

Blasted Heavens

Making Plays by Caridad Svich

Born in Philadelphia, PA to Cuban-Spanish mother and Argentine-Croatian father, I'm a first-generation American living between Spanish and English languages and many cultures. As a child and adolescent, I lived in New Jersey, Florida, Utah, North Carolina, California and New York City. I traveled by car cross-country with my parents twice and I believe that the act of writing stories began for me as I looked at the backyards and back-roads of the US from the backseat of my parents' Chevrolet and listened to the many different voices alive in this beautiful, strange, vast map of a country. Wanderlust is certainly not an uncommon strand in US writing for the stage or otherwise, but what happens to that wanderlust when it bridges not only the US but the Americas and Europe? What kind of text-songs does a writer sing, then?

As a playwright, translator, lyricist, songwriter, essayist, poet, educator, freelance arts journalist and editor over the last twenty years, my commitment to the stage and performance, to the printed word, digital publication, arts advocacy, leadership and mentorship has continually circled around these bridges of land and country, imagined homeland, and eternal road: the metaphorical, spiritual, physical and emotional plain-spoken and weird, twisted songs that make up maps of local and global yearning in a post-post-colonial world.

My work has always, however, centred, whether apparent or not to a less discerning eye, on tracing and creating new maps of seeing theatre and theatre-making, and by extension, seeing the world. All this work has been done as well without a permanent post at an academic institution, and therefore a home base, but rather as an itinerant, freelance artist cobbling together a living. My plays deal principally with migration, exile, the effects of globalisation, celebrity culture and terrorism in the Americas, and the artefacts and remains (and ghosts) of culture – the people and things left behind. My plays over the years have also intersected consistently and powerfully with Greek myth and drama and canonical dramatic texts; there have been free hybrid adaptations and re-imaginings of works by Euripides, Sophocles, Shakespeare, Wedekind, Lope de Vega and Calderon de la Barca.

As a dramatist, in plays such as *Iphigenia Crash Land Falls On the Neon Shell That Was Once Her Heart (a rave fable)*, *12 Ophelias*, *Alchemy of Desire/Dead-Man's Blues*, *Any Place But Here*, *Fugitive Pieces*, *Instructions for Breathing*, and *The Booth Variations, The House of the Spirits* (based on the novel by Isabel Allende) and *In the Time of the Butterflies* (based on the novel by Julia Alvarez), I often work with visual images first as a starting point for creation and draw upon expansive, multilateral layers of hyperlinked research. My approach is to go far and wide into a subject and to discover how patterns emerge and cross-reference themselves politically, emotionally and spiritually through image, word, sound, and music in space and time, from within the actor's body out. How does culture live in the body? How do global and historical currents course through us as human beings, and do not simply live "outside" us?

My work as a writer for the stage, and also as a translator (I've translated nearly all of Federico Garcia Lorca's plays into English as well as works by Julio Cortazar, Lope de Vega, Calderon de la Barca, Antonio Buero Vallejo, and contemporary writers from Mexico, Cuba, Catalonia and Serbia), lyricist/songwriter, arts leader/activist, and editor has focused for many years on how political and erotic bodies are censured, silenced, tortured and treated, and how these bodies find ways to resist tyranny and oppression, prejudice and fear, and contemplate the possibilities of spiritual grace in the modern world. My plays, are often, but not always, set in despoiled landscapes composed of fragments of specifically rooted but consciously blurred geographies and multiple historical time frames that bleed into each other to create a savage, salvaged world: a world of transformation and healing, rising out of, but not always, cruelty, and violence.

The five plays in this collection are central to my aesthetic. The despoiled shores witnessed herein speak to and of merciless heavens and individuals caught in mythic structures, which they either cling to or from which they are finally able to escape. The first two plays *Antigone Arkhe* and *Lucinda Caval* riff on Sophocles' *Antigone* from variant post-modern perspectives. *Steal Back Light from the Virtual* is embedded within the myth of Theseus and the Minotaur and puts on brutal display a cracked-lens world of surveillant dreams, sacrificial bodies and societies adrift in a globalised marketplace where everything, including murder, is for sale. *The Tropic of X* is a cross-gendered, hip-hop, Creole-influenced post-colonial take on the myth of Orpheus and Eurydice. *Wreckage* presents a distaff rendering of Euripides' *Medea* told from the perspective of the murdered sons cycling through stages of their afterlives. All five plays intersect in radical ways with the plays and stories of ancient Greek and Cretan origin, reconfiguring broken worlds in order to discover the bones and phantoms bleeding within.

I'm interested in the remains of/ghosts of culture, and also the inheritances that are borne and marked in our very bones by these remains. I keep coming back too to stories of my family, who have lived through the Balkan wars, Franco's Spain, the dirty war in Argentina, and Castro and Che's revolution in Cuba. My family's many stories are inevitably also part of the memory-scape that ignites the writing process whenever I face the page. Personal, public and fictional histories are bound to collide in the mysterious process that is the creation of a work. Writing for me is always, thus, a kind of archaeological dig – into memory, culture(s), imagination, Eros and the politicized body, and yes, into the lines of poor-rich song that ring out in the land through and past history and real and imagined lives.

Contents

Antigone Arkhe

by

CARIDAD SVICH

Script history:

Antigone Arkhe by Caridad Svich Was originally performed as part of *Antigone Project: A Play in Five Parts,* an evening of works commissioned by Crossing Jamaica Avenue, and co-produced by The Women's Project, New York City in 2004. It was directed by Annie Dorsen.

ANTIGONE ARKHE

ARCHIVIST: An archive is a public building, a place where records are kept. Archival memory may consist of documents, maps, literary texts, letters, archaeological remains, recordings, videos, films, cds, and other ephemera of society.

NARRATION: In the blur of history, in the chaos of memory, words are broken, fragmented, heard anew.

DIGITAL ANTIGONE: Antigone buried the body of her brother. False to him she will never be found.

ARCHIVIST: Thebes (now Thivai), chief city of Boeotia of ancient Greece. Here is the site of the Theban acropolis, part of which still survives. Here lie the remains of a prehistoric city. Right here. Within this caverned rock, within this vault. In a chamber secret as a grave, she was held prisoner.

NARRATION: The litany of the dead is borne here. Listen.

HISTORICAL ANTIGONE: Punish me, brother. Punish my love. For I only loved, and my love costs me. Your body rests, and my body is outside of me. Your body rests, and I wrestle sleep.

ARCHIVIST: In this exhibit you will find: An ivory jewel-box from a chamber tomb of Thebes. A thin belt made of hemp. A simple dress made of silk .A leg torn from a body.

HISTORICAL ANTIGONE: Awaking the ever-new lament in your death you have undone my life. The day-star's sacred eye watches me. Oh city of my fathers in the land of Thebes.

ARCHIVIST: In this exhibit you will find: A statue of a young woman of about human size from the Sanctuary on the mountain. A mirror of undefined origin.

It was here. It was right here where they held her. A caverned rock. A living tomb.

DIGITAL ANTIGONE: Antigone buried her brother. She carried his corpse for miles. She went against every law.

HISTORICAL ANTIGONE: Die I must. I know that well. Even without edicts. But if I am to die before my time, I count that as a gain: for when any one lives as I do, surrounded by evil, can such one find anything but gain in death? These times in which we live, these times of hate, have been lived before. I welcome death if it frees me from these times, and from this well of hate. Accuse me of being Death's bride, and I will accuse you for centuries of going against the laws of heaven, which are beyond time. Make me your martyr. Your power is of this earth, and I am already in heaven.

SCROLL: *ANTIGONE IS LED AWAY BY THE GUARDS.*

NARRATION: Out of earshot, Out of view. Her body quivers

ARCHIVIST: In this exhibit you will find: A map of silence.

Scene 2: Suspension

ARCHIVIST: She used a belt. A thin strap. She hung it from this point right here. You can see a mark where the rock juts out. She took the belt from around her waist and tied it around her neck, and suspended herself from this very point. She knew what she was doing when she spoke out. She buried her brother. That's not technically a crime, but the governor said it was forbidden. There are laws against treason and betrayal. She took his corpse, went out into the public field, buried him, and spoke over his grave, and sang a mournful song. She didn't sing quiet. She wanted the world to hear. So, she got put in here, shoved in like an animal. Creon locked the vault and thought nothing of it.

NARRATION: Antigone lets out a scream before she hangs.

ARCHIVIST: You can't hear anything in here except rain beating. Her uncle Creon put her in here. I think it's worst when it's a family thing. Uncles and brothers and sisters all mixed up in some political tangle...Yes. It was from this point she hung herself. ...Why didn't they take away the belt?... what's a belt worth?...

HISTORICAL ANTIGONE & DIGITAL ANTIGONE: And then I/she stopped screaming, and wept instead, and tasted my/her tears, and tried to move but I/she was tired of wriggling; my/her body was spent. So I/she pretended to be a statue, like those I/she saw at the doors of the sanctuary. I/She was trying to forget how to move. I/She was trying to forget how to speak. I/She was trying to forget how to weep. I/She was trying to forget.

ARCHIVIST: In this exhibit you will find: A thin belt made of hemp. A simple dress made of silk. And a lock of hair.

Interlude: A private recording of Antigone

HISTORICAL ANTIGONE: ...What? Talk into the machine? What do you mean? Closer? Okay. Is this close enough? ...This feels funny. No, it's all right. I'll say things. I'll speak into it. I just don't want my voice to come out wrong. You know? It needs to sound like me. So that if someone were to pick it up and listen, they could say 'hey, that's Antigone. Hey, hey, that's not Johnny, no, that's Antigone"...What? You're recording me now? But I haven't...I'm not ready. I was just... You need a story, right? Something rich and wonderful. Isn't that what you want? Something about my father maybe? I lived with him in exile for years. I was his eyes. My father was a great man. He learned to forget his pride. That's the greatest lesson one could learn in this life...What? Oh. You don't want to hear about my father? ...I can give you something else. What do you want? What do you want from me?}

ARCHIVIST: There seems to have been a malfunction.

HISTORICAL ANTIGONE (FROM RECORDING): What do you -?

ARCHIVIST: There. There. It's over. I'm sorry about that. Machines have lives of their own sometimes. Now, where were we? Ah yes. The belt around her neck. Silence.

DIGITAL ANTIGONE: She was trying to forget how to move. She was trying to forget how to speak. She was trying to forget.

ARCHIVIST: "She must die, and therefore serve the dead eternally, if that is her will." That's what he said. And he led her onto a lonely path, and hid her inside the rocky vault, with barely enough food to last a few days. He thought it the right thing to do. If she was hid, he would avoid public scandal. No one need know where Antigone was sent.

NARRATION: Antigone seeks her tomb. She wishes to be buried in her rightful place. "Where is my bridal chamber? Where is my gown?" she cries.

DIGITAL ANTIGONE: I try to sleep but the siren sounds won't stop. Tighten the noose. Belly up close to thoughts coming in slow motion, suspended:

NARRATION: Creon watches her from his study. He has the inside view. She is his conscience. Best that she is locked up. No one need hear her words of disobedience in this civilized state. In the vault she hangs held inside a frame between marriage and death.

ARCHIVIST: First second

DIGITAL ANTIGONE: Second second

NARRATION: Third...

ARCHIVIST: First second

NARRATION & ARCHIVIST: Second second

ARCHIVIST: Third...

HISTORICAL ANTIGONE: The belt cuts into the neck. Slow torque. Feet kick once against rock. The eyes look up. The flow of oxygen throughout the body stops.

SCROLL: *EXIT ANTIGONE ON THE SPECTATORS' LEFT.*

Scene 3: Altar

SCROLL: *FROM THE CENTRAL DOORS OF THE PALACE.*

ARCHIVIST: An altar is placed for all to see. Antigone is mourned. Objects are left in her name upon the altar. In this exhibit you will find: A pitcher of wine.

A wooden amulet. The petal of dried rose. From this earth you will see: A lacerated neck. Bruised arms. Marks on the tongue. The stuff of legend.

NARRATION: The litany of the dead is borne here. Listen.

DIGITAL ANTIGONE: Swung down, she fell upon the earth

HISTORICAL ANTIGONE: Seven hours later they find me. I am cut down, and laid out on the plain.

DIGITAL ANTIGONE: No more prison-locked is she *THEY CRY*

NARRATION: Beam of the sun, eye of golden day, remember this: our country is the ship that bears us safe, and that only if she thrives in her voyage can we make honest friends.

ARCHIVIST: In this exhibit you will find: A wedding dress from the Hellenistic period. An abject copy of a death decree. A mirror. And a statue of a young woman of about human size.

HISTORICAL ANTIGONE: Here on warm earth stained with blood I walk

DIGITAL ANTIGONE: Under open sky breaking from the heat

HISTORICAL ANTIGONE: One step, and another

DIGITAL ANTIGONE: One girl, and another

HISTORICAL ANTIGONE: Each breath

DIGITAL ANTIGONE: Grants a little more...

HISTORICAL ANTIGONE: And as I look out

DIGITAL ANTIGONE: Beyond the plain, across the open fields

HISTORICAL ANTIGONE: I hear the cries of the living

HISTORICAL ANTIGONE & DIGITAL ANTIGONE: And I touch the skirt of the river with my own bare hands.

Scene 4: Statue

HISTORICAL ANTIGONE: While I rise, and when I rise, the voices of the dead call to me. And I listen. In exile. My body is transferred from Thebes to another city. I watch it as it moves, as one city and another tries to make a place for it. My body travels by ship, and is frozen in time. Someone wants a finger. Someone else wants an eye. Someone steals an eyelash in the night.

DIGITAL ANTIGONE: The tragedy of Antigone is played out on the stage.

ARCHIVIST: In this exhibit you will find...From this earth you will witness:

HISTORICAL ANTIGONE: A young woman about the size of a statue

DIGITAL ANTIGONE: Held up for your scrutiny.

HISTORICAL ANTIGONE: Feel her pulse as she wraps the belt around her neck. Count the minutes it takes for the oxygen to leave her body,

HISTORICAL ANTIGONE & DIGITAL ANTIGONE: First second. Third second. Slow torque...

ARCHIVIST: What's your story, Antigone?

NARRATION: In the blur of history, In the chaos of memory, Words are broken

fragmented, heard anew.

ARCHIVIST: Admit daylight. Admit error. Admit. Confess. Do not stand by ceremony.

HISTORICAL ANTIGONE: And I crawl along the river lit by the moon.

DIGITAL ANTIGONE: And I crawl along the river lit by the moon.

NARRATION: Where is her bridal chamber? Where is her wedding gown?

DIGITAL ANTIGONE & HISTORICAL ANTIGONE: And I drink from the river.

NARRATION: *This is recalled from another time*

DIGITAL ANTIGONE & HISTORICAL ANTIGONE: I drink...

NARRATION: Not long past

DIGITAL ANTIGONE & HISTORICAL ANTIGONE: While I rise, and when I rise, my statue breaks.

ARCHIVIST: Antigone's body has been preserved forever. Her entire body including her brain has been preserved. Some recordings have also been found recently, and while the quality is not good, you can hear Antigone's voice in a special room next to the gift shop as you leave. You can also visit the archaeo-logical museum, and delight in a prehistoric collection, a sculpture collection, a vase collection and a bronze collection from various sites and ancient cemeter-ies. The taking of photographs is strictly prohibited. A new extension to the mu-seum is being planned, pending financial support. We welcome your contribu-tion.

SCROLL: *THE DOORS OF THE PALACE ARE OPENED. THE CORPSE OF ANTI-GONE IS DISCLOSED.*

End of play

LUCINDA CAVAL

(after Sophocles' *Antigone*)

by

CARIDAD SVICH

Script History:

This text was developed through readings at New Dramatists and Primary Stages in New York City, and at Kitchen Dog Theater's New Works Festival in Dallas, Texas. It received a workshop as part of the Women Playwrights Festival co-produced by Seattle Repertory Theatre and Hedgebrook.

This script received the New Dramatists' 2007 Whitfield Cook Prize for New Writing awarded annually to exceptional writing for theatre.

Figures:

LUCINDA CAVAL, strong-willed yet vulnerable woman with a stubborn streak; there is about her a sense of innocence

CLAUDIO, a government functionary, touched by the arrogance of survival; there is about him a sense of wounded-ness

MIREYA, Lucinda's roommate, practical and somewhat chatty, earthbound;

She is a survivor

TOMÁS, a well-regarded architect, recently blinded, sensitive but cutting;

CLERK, in library; also plays CARLOS, Lucinda's fraternal twin brother (on film and live), and JOAN, a transvestite mercenary.

The Setting:

A city of eroded beauty and serene chaos in the aftermath of an uprising that has ushered in a new political order.

Note:

This script should be performed (preferably) with an interval.

Thanks to actors Aysan Celik, Carla Harting, Mercedes Herrero, Marya Sea Kaminski, Gretchen Krich, Lanna Joffrey, Florencia Lozano, Chris McCann, Todd Jefferson Moore, Shanga Parker, Gerardo Rodriguez, Shawn Telford, Michael Tisdale, directors Annie Dorsen, Jean Randich, Val Curtis-Newton, Bruce Coleman and dramaturg Stephen Squibb for being part of the journey; thanks too to Braden Abraham, Elana Greenfield, Stephanie Gilman, and Saviana Stanescu for insights along the way.

Part One

1.

Now. In the hospital, in a gray-white room, Lucinda is seen.

LUCINDA:

My heart stops. They think I'm dead. But I'm not. My eyes are still open and I can see everything: My friend Mireya's hunched shoulders, my brother Carlos' rough hands,

the dirty window-blinds, the sad little light overhead, the itchy hospital linens against my skin, and outside, outside, the blank city,

the terrible city blanketed by terror and signs reading "For sale." *(half-sung)* For sale, all life is for sale; This is the lullaby of the good and gone: For sale. *(spoken)* I can see it all,

while everyone around me thinks I'm dead.

My friend Mireya has a pale blue dress on, very much out of fashion. You can tell she wants everything to end. The sooner to do away with grief and its messy business, the better. My brother Carlos looks away,

towards the city where he'd lost himself,

but his hands reach out to me. I remember our childhood and how we'd been happy

Once, before everything... I think about leaving this earth and what does it all mean.

But I can't think of anything. All I can think about is being safe. Absolutely safe. And then in an instant a thousand lights cut across the sky, and everything goes...

Dark.

2.

Before. The gleaming library, now defunct, is a temporary office of records.
Lucinda faces Claudio.

LUCINDA: I just want to know where he is.

CLAUDIO: Who?

LUCINDA: My brother.

CLAUDIO: What's his name again?

LUCINDA: Carlos. Carlos de la Torre.

CLAUDIO: De la Torre....Doesn't ring.

LUCINDA: What about Reyes? Maybe he's under Reyes.

CLAUDIO: What do you mean?

LUCINDA: Sometimes he'd use that name.

CLAUDIO: Why would he do that?

LUCINDA: It's a family name. Some people knew him by that name.

CLAUDIO: There's no Reyes here.

LUCINDA: You haven't even looked.

CLAUDIO: I remember everyone. All the names.

LUCINDA: Reyes is a common name.

CLAUDIO: It hasn't come up.

LUCINDA: What does that mean?

CLAUDIO: Means what it means.

LUCINDA: ...You don't want to help me.

CLAUDIO: Are you accusing me of not doing my job?

LUCINDA: No. I'm sorry. I know you're...

CLAUDIO: I'm doing my best.

LUCINDA: Yes. I realize that. I'm sorry.

I just want to know where my brother is.

CLAUDIO: I can't do anything for you until you've filled out the form.

LUCINDA: I've filled out every form there is.

CLAUDIO: You'll have to wait, then.

LUCINDA: I've been waiting. I've waited for weeks.

CLAUDIO: You have to be patient. You're not the only one, Miss.

LUCINDA: Caval. Lucinda Caval.

CLAUDIO: ...Is that a Catholic name?

LUCINDA: What?

CLAUDIO: Are you Catholic?

LUCINDA: No.

CLAUDIO: Christian, then?

LUCINDA: Sure.

CLAUDIO: You don't sound convinced.

LUCINDA: I don't think about religion very much anymore.

CLAUDIO: Why not?

LUCINDA: ...It doesn't enter in somehow.

CLAUDIO: We should all pray. For the good of this country. For the good of the world.

LUCINDA: ...If you would just look under Caval. C-A-V-V as in Victor - A-L. Lucinda.

My name has to be there. My forms have been floating through this office for weeks.

CLAUDIO: Yes, well... I'm new here.

LUCINDA: Everyone's new here. (And they don't know shit.)

CLAUDIO: There's no need for that language. See the sign?

LUCINDA: What sign?

CLAUDIO: There. Look up.

A discreetly embedded electronic scroll that repeatedly reads "#$&%" is revealed on one of the walls of the office of records.

LUCINDA: That's new.

CLAUDIO: We're making every effort to make this a cleaner, better place. Clean streets, clean language... clean everything.

LUCINDA: I just want my brother back.

CLAUDIO: ...Carlos Reyes?

LUCINDA: Yes.

CLAUDIO: Carlos de la Torre? *[She nods.]* You've filled out forms with both names?

LUCINDA: Yes.

CLAUDIO: You should fill out one form and one form only with one name and an alias.

If you fill out the form properly, it will expedite the process on all sides. Here. Take this form. Once you fill it out, we can get things in order.

LUCINDA: ...I've already filled this form out.

CLAUDIO: Fill it out again.

LUCINDA: Can't you just...? I know I'm there. In the files. I have to be... Lucinda Caval.

The man who was here before... he knew me.

He used to work in this building when it was a library. You can ask him. I come from a good family. We've never caused any trouble of any kind. This library was like our home. My brother and I would come here and read for hours. We'd trace the words on the pages with our hands. Sometimes we'd be here so long we'd forget what time it was.

CLAUDIO: Tracing words?

LUCINDA: It was nothing. Fingers on pages...when we were children.

CLAUDIO: I see.

LUCINDA: *[looking at small stack off to one side]* Is that all that's left now?

CLAUDIO: Only what's allowed: *Great Expectations, Call of the Wild*, and Hitchcock's 'Vertigo." Have you seen it?

LUCINDA: No.

CLAUDIO: You should see it. Kim Novak...

LUCINDA: Who?

CLAUDIO: Actress. In the movie. Reminds me of you a bit.

LUCINDA: Really?

CLAUDIO: Just something about your eyes. ...Caval... Is it your husband's surname?

LUCINDA: I'm not married.

CLAUDIO: Why not?

LUCINDA: It's not a crime, is it?

CLAUDIO: No, but it's a shame...

LUCINDA: ...Caval's a family name

CLAUDIO: You've a big family. De la Torre, Reyes...

LUCINDA: Everyone's dead.

CLAUDIO: Except for your brother, eh?

LUCINDA: If that's what your records say.

CLAUDIO: My records don't say anything. They don't speak.

LUCINDA: Please...don't play games with me.

CLAUDIO: Is that what you think I'm doing?

LUCINDA: I don't know what to think. I've been coming here talking to you people for....

Every day there's a different person; every day there's a different form. And I wait and wait and nothing...

CLAUDIO: You're frustrated. I can see that.

LUCINDA: You're not listening to me.

CLAUDIO: I've heard everything you said, Ms. Caval. I pride myself on doing my job. And doing it well. I don't know who you've been dealing with before, but I'm not like them. I listen. See? I actually give a fuck.

LUCINDA: You're allowed to curse here?

CLAUDIO: Twice a day. Rules for you and rules for me. See? Now, about your brother....

I think maybe what it is... perhaps it hasn't occurred to you...Ms. Caval, have you ever thought it could be that he doesn't want to be found? Maybe your brother's run away, abandoned his life here. People do that, you know. They've been doing that for quite a while.

LUCINDA: He wouldn't do that.

CLAUDIO: How do you know? What do you know of anything? He could be anywhere.

LUCINDA: ...You won't help me.

CLAUDIO: Ms. Caval, I will help you, but you have to... I want to help you. Believe me.

But you should also think about other scenarios...After all, we can only do so much in this world.

LUCINDA: ...Give me back his photo.

CLAUDIO: Sorry?

LUCINDA: ...The photo I gave you when I came in.

CLAUDIO: We need something to...

LUCINDA: You don't need anything. Your mind's made up. Carlos doesn't exist. He's lost and that's it.

CLAUDIO: Ms. Caval.

LUCINDA: I want my brother back.

CLAUDIO: ...You have to wait.

LUCINDA: How long?

Silence.

CLAUDIO: I'm an ordinary man doing an ordinary job. This is my desk. For today. And if I do my job well, for tomorrow too. You see?

But you have to be patient with me. You have to trust me, Ms. Caval. I can't do anything without trust. I'll locate your brother. I promise I'll do the best I can. Come back in a fortnight. Ask for me: Claudio. Just Claudio for now. The rest will come later.

3.

In the run-down apartment,

Mireya drinks tea, while Lucinda searches in a box.

MIREYA: Did he say what time?

LUCINDA: He said in a fortnight, that's all.

MIREYA: And you believed him?

LUCINDA: What choice do I have?

MIREYA: He could have you waiting for him all day once you're there. They're like that, you know, those government types...

LUCINDA: Mireya, he's a clerk.

MIREYA: So? He's a government type all the same. Well, we all are now, in a manner of speaking. We all move to the same compass.

LUCINDA: Because we have to.

MIREYA: I don't mind. I like order. Keeps people out of trouble. ...What are you looking for?

LUCINDA: I thought I had another photo...

MIREYA: Of Carlos?

LUCINDA: *(searching)* I don't know where I...

MIREYA: Did you look in the box?

LUCINDA: What do you think I'm doing?

MIREYA: The other box. In the closet. The one with all the junk in it.

LUCINDA: I already looked. There's nothing. ...I shouldn't have given it to him.

MIREYA: You don't need a photo. You've Carlos in mind. What's a photo going to do?

LUCINDA: I should learn to live with nothing, is that it? Adhere to the new doctrine?

MIREYA: A photo's just a piece of paper. It's in the past. A thing of the past.

LUCINDA: It was the last thing I had of Carlos.

MIREYA: Well, ask the clerk for it when you see him again.

LUCINDA: ...No.

MIREYA: Have some tea, then. Come on. Calm down.

LUCINDA: I'm all right.

MIREYA: You're moving around. You're making me nervous.

LUCINDA: *(locating item in box)* There. You see. I knew it. I knew I had.... shit.

MIREYA: What is it?

LUCINDA: The photo's been torn in half.

MIREYA: Maybe it was always like that.

LUCINDA: It wasn't always like this. I remember. I remember when this picture was taken. Carlos and I had gone to the zoo, when it was still open. We walked for hours looking at the all the animals that were still left. He said: we'll stand here next to the giraffe. He loved giraffes. He asked a woman in a red coat to take our picture. He didn't know her. She was from another city. But very kind. Warm smile. Carlos would always mention her when he'd look at this picture. Someone came in here, Mireya. Someone came in here...and cut him out.

MIREYA: Nobody did anything.

LUCINDA: How did it happen, then? ....They take everything away from us: Our books, stories, buildings...people... *(She tears to bits what's left of the photo.)* Well, now they have nothing. Absolutely nothing.

MIREYA: ...You want some tea?

LUCINDA: ...It's awful.

MIREYA: It's all there is. ...

Lucinda sits, and drinks tea.

LUCINDA: ...Oo-long. Carlos and I would have Oo-long tea when we came from school. We'd take turns reading the leaves.

MIREYA: In my house, we'd read coffee grinds. With my Auntie Lena. She had the gift, you know. Every time she'd read the grounds, we'd be in fear of what she'd say. Don't make it be true, we'd say. Or Make it be true, if it was a good thing. And Auntie Lena... she'd just smile. Full of secrets. I wanted to be just like her. When I was a child. Auntie Lena was my ideal. Strange what we think about, eh? As children. Strange thoughts enter our brains and enchant us. It's a kind of poison, I think...benevolent poison, but poison nonetheless. Why be seduced by such enchantment? Who was Auntie Lena anyway but an odd, unmarried woman who wore bright red lipstick and painted her nails a sallow shade of pink? And to think that's who I wanted to be! I can't even imagine it. But why think about all that? Memories are of no use.

LUCINDA: They're all we have.

MIREYA: They mess up your brain, confuse things...

Now's all there is, and the sooner we convince ourselves of that, the better. ...You're going to Tomás' place later?

LUCINDA: Yes.

MIREYA: I don't know how he lives his life. Tomás was such a brilliant man.

LUCINDA: Still is.

MIREYA: Of course, but you know what I mean... He's not altogether there, is he?

Not the same as before. I mean, Tomás was one of those lights: celebrated architect, in the news and all that; he was quite a figure, and now what? He's lost his sight and turned into a shut-in.

LUCINDA: Not completely.

MIREYA: But he's reclusive.

LUCINDA: He's just finding his way.

MIREYA: All I know is he's lucky he has you stopping in, checking in with him.

LUCINDA: It's a job.

MIREYA: Good job. How many people would like a job like that: being a reader? With all the shit-work and no work that's out there... at least you've something. ...Which of the two books is it tonight?

LUCINDA: *Great Expectations.*

MIREYA: Tomás likes that one, eh?

LUCINDA: It's an exemplary story of caution and survival.

MIREYA: What's that?

LUCINDA: It's what they said, isn't it, when they got rid of everything else except *Great Expectations* and the *Call of the Wild.*

MIREYA: And "Vertigo." Have you seen it?

The soap opera on channel 2 is based on it. It's good.

LUCINDA: Sometimes I think where'd they put all the rest of them. They couldn't have burned all the books...erased everything..

Somebody somewhere must've salvaged something. Scraps, right? I bet there are scraps of lost books hidden all over this city. Just have to know where to look...

MIREYA: No point in that.

LUCINDA: Don't worry. I won't go looking, Mireya.

MIREYA: That's not what I meant.

LUCINDA: What'd you mean, then?

MIREYA: The stories we've been left with are good enough. Tomás likes *Great Expectations*, right?

LUCINDA: Sure, but most of it's been cut out.

When I read to him, I spend half my time filling in the gaps.

MIREYA: There's no filling in the gaps. You know that.

LUCINDA: Well, I can't read it to him as is.

MIREYA: What if somebody else hears you?

LUCINDA: Let them. They probably don't know what I'm making up anyway.

MIREYA: You should be more careful. You think things are safe now? The death workers are still out there.

LUCINDA: Outside the gates. Yes.

MIREYA: And inside too. Just because we've gated zones now doesn't mean it's all peace and goddamn quiet. I mean, it's better. Yeah.

But it doesn't mean a bomb can't blast through one building or another at any given time. You saw what happened to Letty's grocery store the other day.

LUCINDA: It was awful. All that glass, all that blood...

MIREYA: And not even five blocks away. I tell you, sometimes it's best just to accept things as they are. Forget what was part of a story... Let things go, you know.

LUCINDA: ...Let Carlos go? Is that what you're saying? Carlos and I were left together very young. We had no one else. We raised each other.

MIREYA: Orphaned, fraternal twins. Yes. I know.

LUCINDA: I had no one else, Mireya. I have no one else.

MIREYA: ...Look, we made a pact, right? After the war, we all said it's best if there was no more talk of before, of the things that happened...

LUCINDA: And keep happening.

MIREYA: A pact of forgetting. For the good of us all.

LUCINDA: Clean slate society? I can't live like that.

MIREYA: I know it hurts. Christ. I know...all this business with your brother and...

LUCINDA: Business? What business? We were in the old mall mindlessly looking at crap,

and the next thing I know is he's gone.

Vanished. We'd been right next to each other not even a minute before. He goes down one aisle, I go down another, and that's it. I never see him again. ... And it wasn't like there was a tussle or a scream or...just silence, right?

Nobody sees anything, hears anything, knows anything.

MIREYA: If we stay in memory, we'll lose ourselves.

LUCINDA: What's that? More doctrine? What the hell's happened to you? You used to believe in things. You used to march in the streets. Remember? Spit on the pigs.

MIREYA: But at day's end, what? What did we achieve? Nothing but screwy idealistic left of center trademark bullshit behavior; fucking cliches, we were. Fucking whiny ideologues high on our own righteousness and passion. And the truth is, all that marching and crap, it wasn't even me. I mean, I believed in things, but results? Did I really think the whole world was going to change just because I spit on some pig? No. And I know now I shouldn't have. It would've been more sensible to just wait things out. Like everybody else. Hell. We're all the same now. All in the same fucking boat. What's all the going-round-in-your-head-trying-to-figure-things-out going to do? It won't bring Carlos back.

LUCINDA: Carlos isn't dead.

MIREYA: You don't know that.

LUCINDA: Precisely. I don't know.

MIREYA: You should get it into your head. I mean, it's been what? Months now.

LUCINDA: Doesn't mean he's dead. Some people have been...

MIREYA: ... they're not Carlos.

LUCINDA: Meaning?

MIREYA: He shouldn't have said all those things. That time.

LUCINDA: What are you talking about?

MIREYA: At the mayor's office.

LUCINDA: We were all there, Mireya. It wasn't just Carlos.

MIREYA: No, but his voice... it rung out.

LUCINDA: We hadn't had water for three months. It wasn't like we were asking for something special. Basic needs, you know...

Are you saying he deserved to be kidnapped?

MIREYA: No. But...his words...

LUCINDA: He said what he felt was right at the time. "Butcher the butcher." Everyone was saying it. Not just Carlos. Everyone said that about the mayor. On the walls, in graffiti...It was everywhere. Don't you remember? It was a phrase... a stupid phrase...that's all. ...If he's dead (Have mercy on him), I want his body. I've the right to bury him. As family. His only family.

MIREYA: You've every right in the world. Absolutely. All I'm saying is...looking for people that are gone won't change who we are now.

LUCINDA: ...Someone's threatened you.

MIREYA: No, but people talk, that's all.

LUCINDA: And you feed their talk, right?

MIREYA: What have I to feed them with? Tea?

You think I like living like this? I had a house, right? I had my own things, things I'd worked my whole life for. And one day, they took it away and put me here in this little apartment.

Go share a room, they said, like everyone else.

There won't be any privileges here. And when I saw it was you they'd paired me up with, I said, Well, at least it's someone I know, someone I can trust. Lucinda, I'm your friend. All I'm trying to do is to help you. ...What happens if you get put away? You ever think about that? What happens to me? ... You're on your little crusade and screw the rest, eh? Well let me tell you, honey, I'm already screwed. But I put up with it, cause I love my country. I love it to death.

LUCINDA: ...I should go to Tomás.

MIREYA: Go. Go on. Read your lousy book.

LUCINDA: You don't have to stay up for me.

MIREYA: It's the tea, honey. You know that. It's the tea that keeps me up.

4.

*In the small apartment between the alleys, Tomás is seated in an old chair. His back is to the window. He is blind. Lucinda sits in a low chair with book in hand. She reads to him [from chapter 47 of **Great Expectations**]:*

LUCINDA: "It was in those very moments when he was closest to me...I should be so unconscious and off my guard...as if I had shut an avenue of hundred doors to keep him out, and then...found him at my elbow."

TOMÁS: ...Why'd you stop?

LUCINDA: I thought I heard something.

TOMÁS: Outside?

LUCINDA: ...It's nothing.

TOMÁS: There were shots earlier. Before you came. Far off. But I could hear them.

LUCINDA: Routine?

TOMÁS: Could have been. Or maybe a celebration.

LUCINDA: What'd you mean?

TOMÁS: A wedding. Shots in the air for happiness. For love. People still get married, don't they?

LUCINDA: Yes. Of course.

TOMÁS: ...Sometimes when it's too quiet, I get worried. I'd rather noise.

LUCINDA: Even shots?

TOMÁS: Even if it's murder. Yes. Do you think me strange?

LUCINDA: I've no opinion.

TOMÁS: You don't convince me.

LUCINDA: I think we're all different, and are asked to think alike.... Should I pick up where I left off?

TOMÁS: Lucinda, every day you come here and read to me and I listen and pretend I have no feeling. Now, I admit that at first, I didn't. I resented that you came. You were simply another job-seeker, someone who answered an advert to become a reader, to become an odd sort of literary companion to a rather desperate, frightened man. But time has passed. Enough time that I know every line of what's left of *Great Expectations*, and can detect with every reading how your day has been, and what this shifting world we're in is like.

And yet every day you close the book as if no time has passed, as if you're still just a reader, and there was no history between us, and you say Good morning, Tomás, Good evening, Tomás. Cordial, sweet. Perhaps with a trace of pity. But not endearing. Not in the least.

And I'm left, you see? I'm left here thinking about you. About what you might be wearing. About the way you smell. About the softness of your voice even when you're trying so very much to be hard. And I keep thinking When are we going to drop all this pretense? When are we going to leave Dickens and Jack London to one side and just talk to each other, just be with each other like two relatively ordinary human beings waiting out the night?

LUCINDA: ...I should go.

TOMÁS: You've only just arrived.

LUCINDA: You've lost track of time. It's getting late. The whole street will be shut down soon.

TOMÁS: Don't lie to me. I know when the street shuts down. I know all the sounds.

LUCINDA: I wouldn't lie to you, Tomás.

TOMÁS: But you won't talk to me, is that it? Weather, yes. Safety, yes. But not a real conversation. Or is it that you can only have one through books? Through the toleration of old stories and their winding paragraphs of loss? You sit and read and count the words and trace them with your fingers (I hear your fingertips across the pages) and you wrap phrases around your mouth as if the memory of those phrases could change things

as they are now and will be for some time in this world we live in, this interrupted world full of cries and furtive glances I can't see

but feel...all around...yes...and yet you hide behind these words, these remnants of the past, fallen letters from old dilapidated buildings whose girders are about to break because you think these old words are safe; that they'll protect you somehow, that they'll protect us, when they won't. They can't.

They have no power against the avenues that shut down at midnight, and the shots that keep firing long after you're asleep. I hear them, you see? I hear everything.

LUCINDA: ...I'll come back tomorrow when you've...

TOMÁS: Settled down? I'm perfectly settled.

[*quoting from memory a line from* Great Expectations] "unspeakable trouble...considered and reconsidered...at last dissolve that spell of my childhood..." I've nowhere to go. My life is to sit here in this damned apartment and listen to everything that goes on outside my window.

LUCINDA: You can do other things.

TOMÁS: Yes. I can walk down stairs, take a stroll. Count the steps. Listen, listen, listen... to whispers and murmurs and sad dogs barking

and gunshots and occasional screams and children, little children, singing songs of hatred as they make their way back home from school, and all the while, I imagine how the neighborhood must look now after everything,

after all the chaos and the fires and I try to remember what this city was like when I was a child but I can't remember. All I remember is the country – ridiculous days spent in the country with vaguely friendly relatives who wanted nothing more than to get rid of me.

LUCINDA: You want me to tell you what the city is like?

TOMÁS: Only if you can tell me without words. (*Silence.*) Lucinda?

LUCINDA: Yes.

TOMÁS: What are you doing?

LUCINDA: I'm taking off my clothes.

TOMÁS: Lucinda...

LUCINDA: Shh.

She kisses him.

TOMÁS: ...I don't know why I'm crying.

She caresses him.

LUCINDA: ...It gets dark so early now.

TOMÁS: When I was a child, it was always light.

They begin to make love.

5.

The office of records, which was formerly the library,

is lit by a slim shaft of light.

A surveillance camera rotates slightly catching Lucinda as she walks in.

Lucinda sits in a chair, and waits. Silence.

Hours go by.

The incessant electronic hum of surveillance becomes unbearable,

as Lucinda listens to what seems to be a whispered, emotionless scroll of all the names of the missing echoing through the library.

Lucinda rises and approaches the main desk.

A clerk appears, seemingly out of nowhere.

CLERK: What are you doing?

LUCINDA: I was... I was told to come here.

CLERK: Who sent you?

LUCINDA: Sorry?

CLERK: Have you been sent?

LUCINDA: No, I... I was here two weeks ago. I was told to come back.

CLERK: Who told you that?

LUCINDA: Claudio.

CLERK: Who?

LUCINDA: I don't...Just Claudio.

CLERK: There's no one here by that name.

LUCINDA: Two weeks ago he –

CLERK: This office has been closed for three weeks.

LUCINDA: I spoke to... Claudio. He told me to come back. He was very clear. See that small stack over there? It was there two weeks ago.

In exactly the same place. I wouldn't forget a thing like that. I've a good memory. *Great Expectations, Call of the Wild,* "Vertigo."

I remember everything.

CLERK: You imagine everything.

LUCINDA: …He's very handsome. Like you.

CLERK: Brazen girl. Put my hand in?

LUCINDA: If you like.

CLERK: This your game?

LUCINDA: No game.

CLERK: Just because you want, then? You like me?

LUCINDA: Yes.

CLERK: *(he moves in, discreetly)* What's that smell?

LUCINDA: Nothing.

CLERK: Lavender.

LUCINDA: It's nothing.

CLERK: Soap, eh? You like cleaning yourself up?

LUCINDA: No.

CLERK: Dirty girl. Filthy girl.

LUCINDA: Yes.

CLERK: I should hit you.

LUCINDA: That your game?

CLERK: Back of the hand, straight across the face, yeah.

LUCINDA: Maybe later.

CLERK: What'd you say his name was again?

LUCINDA: Claudio.

CLERK: …Yes.

LUCINDA: You remember now?

CLERK: *(breaking away)* He's gone.

LUCINDA: What?

CLERK: There's no one here for you. No one at all. Get a move on. ...Out! *(She walks away. She's almost gone when...he reveals small envelope)* Hey. You left this.

LUCINDA: What?

CLERK: This. Fell out of your bag while you were waiting.

LUCINDA: No, I didn't...

CLERK: Don't contradict me. *(Clerk holds out envelope. Lucinda understands the envelope is meant for her, and takes it.)* You should be more careful, Miss. Don't know what would've happened if I hadn't been here.

LUCINDA: Yes. Thank you.

CLERK: I'm here to serve, that's all.

6.

The empty movie theater. Lucinda walks in. Silence.

LUCINDA: Claudio? ...Claudio?

CLAUDIO: *(revealed)* I'm right here.

LUCINDA: It is you.

CLAUDIO: The note said I'd be here; I'm here.

I'm true to my word, Lucinda. You should know that about me. Faith, right? It's all we have in the end. Did anyone see you -?

LUCINDA: The streets are empty.

CLAUDIO: Filchers, though.

LUCINDA: The filchers aren't round here.

CLAUDIO: They will be. Those that sell whatever's needed always show up to do their trade.

LUCINDA: Arrest them.

CLAUDIO: It's not my job.

LUCINDA: You stay to your job?

CLAUDIO: Yes.

LUCINDA: So, have you found something?

About my brother?

CLAUDIO: ...I want to help, you know. I want to help you. I understand what it's like.

LUCINDA: Why here?

CLAUDIO: I like the movies.

LUCINDA: This place is a wreck.

CLAUDIO: Decadent, though. Cheap, decadent movie palace. Can't beat that.

Besides, it'll be knocked down soon. It's our last chance to experience it in all its battered glory.

LUCINDA: Why do you talk like that?

CLAUDIO: Like what?

LUCINDA: Like a movie.

CLAUDIO: I told you. I like them.

LUCINDA: "Vertigo?"

CLAUDIO: You've seen it?

LUCINDA: No.

CLAUDIO: You should.

LUCINDA: What are they going to put here? What's this place going to be?

CLAUDIO: Probably a government building.

Or some sort of monument.

LUCINDA: To war?

CLAUDIO: To victory. New buildings are a defining characteristic of healthy civilizations.

Architecture stimulates society, culture and the economy.

LUCINDA: You sound like a brochure.

CLAUDIO: I thought you said I sounded like a movie.

LUCINDA: I hate movies. The only stories I like are in books.

CLAUDIO: The books that are gone, I suppose.

LUCINDA: The ones that have been forever erased by your government.

CLAUDIO: Yours, too. There's only one side now, remember?

LUCINDA: Yes.

CLAUDIO: You should be more careful. You should watch yourself.

LUCINDA: Am I being watched?

CLAUDIO: Not here.

LUCINDA: Why not?

CLAUDIO: It's safe here. Nobody cares about this place. It's a dead building.

LUCINDA: Ghost palace.

CLAUDIO: Good name for it.

LUCINDA: Like the rest of this city.

CLAUDIO: Ghosts go away.

LUCINDA: They linger.

CLAUDIO: Shake them off.

LUCINDA: I can't. My memory's too good.

CLAUDIO: There are drugs for that. I'll get you some. I want to protect you.

LUCINDA: Why?

CLAUDIO: Compassion. Pity. Solidarity.

LUCINDA: You've lost someone, too.

CLAUDIO: My wife.

LUCINDA: I'm sorry.

CLAUDIO: We used to come here. To this place. She loved the movies. We'd get ice cream and sit way up in the balcony like we were children all over again. It's the only place we could really...be ourselves.

LUCINDA: I'm sorry. I thought...

CLAUDIO: What? That government types were exempt from loss? We're like anyone else. In power, sure. Job, sure. But for how long?

They could put me to the trash from one day to the next. I'm no different than you. You remind me of my wife. She had your temper.

LUCINDA: I don't have a temper.

CLAUDIO: You have character.

LUCINDA: Meaning?

CLAUDIO: You say what you mean.

LUCINDA: I don't.

CLAUDIO: You lie?

LUCINDA: No. But I don't always say what I mean. It's not smart.

CLAUDIO: And you're smart?

LUCINDA: Sometimes.

CLAUDIO: Which is why you're here.

LUCINDA: I don't know if this is smart.

CLAUDIO: Being here or being with me?

LUCINDA: Both.

CLAUDIO: You did the right thing taking that envelope.

LUCINDA: He almost didn't give it to me.

CLAUDIO: He's a good clerk.

LUCINDA: He said he'd never heard of you.

CLAUDIO: He says what he's told to say.

LUCINDA: He said you'd been sacked.

CLAUDIO: He used that word specifically?

LUCINDA: No. He said "gone."

CLAUDIO: Well, I am gone. I've been promoted.

LUCINDA: Just like that?

CLAUDIO: I'm a good worker.

LUCINDA: So, what's your new job?

CLAUDIO: This.

LUCINDA: Guarding an old movie theater?

CLAUDIO: ...Do you always smell like that?

LUCINDA: What?

CLAUDIO: Lavender. I miss fragrances. Perfumes...

LUCINDA: ...Do they remind you of your wife?

CLAUDIO: Yes.

LUCINDA: How'd she...?

CLAUDIO: She was taken. From our house. Men in cheap clothes came in and took her one day. They said she violated some new statute. Which one I'll never know. They've made sure to keep me in the dark about that.

LUCINDA: I'm sorry.

CLAUDIO: It doesn't make any sense, really. My wife was a reporter. She wrote the party line. Never strayed. She was good at her job, too. Never questioned. She had a sixth sense, if you will, for divining the next new party line.

So, you see, the fact of these men...coming to our house,

LUCINDA: You saw them?

CLAUDIO: I let them in. I let them...hit her.

They had a gun to my head. I had to let them.

They hit her quite a bit. With their fists. One of them had a ring. Huge ring. He did the most damage. They made me watch. They wouldn't let me move. Two of them had me firm in their grip. They said they'd kill me. I believed them. I had no choice. They kept hitting her. She was angry at me. She wanted me to die for her. But

I couldn't. I was selfish. I wanted to protect myself. So I watched as they tied her up, bound her wrists and ankles with my neckties.

She was barely conscious from their beating.

She didn't have the strength to scream but they gagged her anyway. They stuffed her mouth with a pair of stockings. It was all very crude.

I'm sure they wanted to use our personal things – neckties, stockings - as a way of inflicting subtle psychological damage.

It's something I've come to learn.

LUCINDA: Strategies for doing damage?

CLAUDIO: It's not something I'm proud of. It's just knowledge. Rather painful knowledge, if you want to know the truth.

LUCINDA: And she...?

CLAUDIO: They took her away. I never saw her again.

LUCINDA: Have you tried –?

CLAUDIO: Everything. No sign.

LUCINDA: I'm sorry.

CLAUDIO: ...I live with what I live with.

LUCINDA: ...As should I? Is that what you mean?

CLAUDIO: ... I lost someone that I loved. I thought you'd understand.

LUCINDA: We're the same? We're not.

You see, I'd die for Carlos. I wouldn't stand by and watch.

CLAUDIO: You don't know that.

LUCINDA: I do. Absolutely.

CLAUDIO: Words...Limpid...languid...liquid (words)... nothing but phantoms.

LUCINDA: ...I won't stop looking for Carlos.

CLAUDIO: Which is why you're here with me instead of being with Tomás. You think I don't know?

LUCINDA: You are watching me.

CLAUDIO: Our culture is built on surveillance.

LUCINDA: Poor culture.

CLAUDIO: Is that what you think?

LUCINDA: I don't think anything. I'm a good citizen.

CLAUDIO: Brazen girl.

LUCINDA: Those were his words, too.

CLAUDIO: Whose?

LUCINDA: The man who works for you, the clerk, the one you trained.

CLAUDIO: I don't train anybody.

LUCINDA: Must be someone else, then.

CLAUDIO: Higher up. Yes.

LUCINDA: You're low on the ladder?

CLAUDIO: There's no ladder here.

LUCINDA: Fair culture?

CLAUDIO: Yes. It is. You think differently?

LUCINDA: I don't think anything. I told you.

CLAUDIO: Blank woman?

LUCINDA: If you like.

CLAUDIO: How do you know what I like?

LUCINDA: I can guess.

CLAUDIO: Shouldn't do that.

LUCINDA: Not allowed?

CLAUDIO: Not preferred. No.

LUCINDA: May I ask you a question, then?

CLAUDIO: I'm here to serve. You know that.

LUCINDA: Are you all trained to stick your hands in?

CLAUDIO: I don't know what you mean.

LUCINDA: You know perfectly. You were watching me. At the office of records.

CLAUDIO: I haven't been to the office of records in a fortnight.

LUCINDA: Your surveillance capacity is limited?

CLAUDIO: I'm only human.

LUCINDA: What about here?

CLAUDIO: This is a safe place. Off-limits.

LUCINDA: Why?

CLAUDIO: Nobody cares about the movies.

LUCINDA: You're full of shit.

CLAUDIO: Language.

LUCINDA: Is there a sign?

CLAUDIO: No.

LUCINDA: Then I'll curse all I like. How much did you fucking see? The clerk and me?

CLAUDIO: Nothing.

LUCINDA: What about Tomás and me?

CLAUDIO: What do you care?

LUCINDA: I read to him. It's my job.

CLAUDIO: I think everyone deserves to be loved.

LUCINDA: I don't love him.

CLAUDIO: Look, what goes on between you and Tomás – Doesn't concern me. I just want him to be happy. We were friends once. And I still care for him, despite the accident.

LUCINDA: What accident?

CLAUDIO: His eyes.

LUCINDA: Were you responsible for that?

CLAUDIO: Look, let's keep things simple.

You want to find your brother. I'm here to help you. Not because I care. I don't. But I empathize, okay? I'm making an effort outside my jurisdiction, let's say. Because what I don't want is for people like you to think I'm,

That this government, is unfeeling. I know there have been plenty of cases...loads of people unaccounted for, my wife included, and well, it's not something I like living with necessarily. And I can imagine, it's not something you want to live with for the rest of your life: this not knowing, This unease, disease...am I right?

LUCINDA: Yes.

CLAUDIO: Right. So, you can think what you like... you can hate me, if that's what you want... (One must learn how to hate, after all.

It's part of any society that thrives) but when we're here, like this, on my time, we'll have to trust each other. And if you think there's someone else who's going to help you,

who's going to actually give a fuck, you're quite mistaken. I'm all you have. And if you don't believe me, go out there, knock on the damn doors that won't open, have some terrorist manqué grab you in the middle of the street, put a hood over your head and shoot you for nothing. Believe me, that can be arranged. Easier than you think. Do you understand?

LUCINDA: Yes.

CLAUDIO: ...He goes by Reyes, right?

LUCINDA: Carlos Reyes. Yes. Sometimes.

CLAUDIO: I've been able to trace...

LUCINDA: What?

CLAUDIO: It's not definite, you understand. It may not be him.

LUCINDA: Where is he? Tell me.

CLAUDIO: This is all I have.

Claudio clicks a remote device. A digital moving image comes up on the movie screen: fragmented and shifting images of Carlo's face, wearing opaque sunglasses. Close-up of lower left portion of his face, then his lips, then straight-on close-up of his face. Freeze.

LUCINDA: Carlos...

CLAUDIO: There's a bit of his voice here, too...

Image unfreezes. Still in close-up, Carlos' voice comes up:

CARLOS: It's okay. Yeah. I'm okay. It's nice...here.

Image shifts away from Carlos abruptly to a pool in the background and greenery. An idyllic image.

(VO) I like the pool. It's real blue, not fake shit. It's cool.

LUCINDA: He sounds happy.

The shot lingers for a moment then shifts back to medium shot of Carlos standing in a room in a villa. He wears bright T-shirt and jeans in addition to the sunglasses. He waves to the camera.

He always used to do that.

Wave. Whenever I'd take a picture of him. Waving to the ghosts, he'd say.

CLAUDIO: What ghosts?

CARLOS: I'm okay. Sure. I'm happy. What?

Camera closes in on Carlos' face then shifts abruptly away and focuses on wall of room in the villa. Extended VO: rough noise and the sound of Carlos being beaten; his shouts are muffled. Image cuts out.

LUCINDA: What's happened to him? ...Claudio?

Claudio is gone. Dark.

Part Two

7.

Now. In the gray-white room of the hospital, Lucinda is seen.

LUCINDA: I pretend I'm invisible. It's a game Carlos and I used to play when we were little.

I always won. I was better at it than he was. I still am. Even here, where everyone can see me....I'm unseen. They all think I'm dead. They speak in whispers. They look away.

They write things down on a sheet of paper with my name on it. They call for a priest even though I'm not Catholic. They say it's time for prayer. Blessings on the dead. What blessings do I deserve? I've lived a mediocre life. Carlos may think of me as the best sister in the world, but I'm not even close. I failed him, you see? I'm still failing him. Even here, when I should be reaching out and holding his hand, I keep in my pretense. I choose invisibility. Carlos used to say I liked being protected from things, protected from knowing. But he doesn't understand: what I like is the illusion of protection.

The priest arrives. He looks as if he's been dragged out of some hole. He's wearing an awful suit and his breath smells. He hovers over me but he can't see me either. To him, I'm just another body. Just another job. He starts to pray. Useless words in Latin. He has an owl's face. I want to pinch it. But I don't. I lie still. I play dead. I let him finish his side of the story.

After all, he's probably getting paid something by somebody to bless me. I don't want him to lose what little he can make now.

Carlos watches me. He's standing to one side, looking bored. He's not even crying. Maybe he's pretending, too. Maybe he wants to beat me in this game of invisibility. When we were little, we used to dream about sailing off on a magical boat made up of all the lost books in the world. In our dream we'd float over the endless ocean and live off of the torn pages and banished words and no one would ever find us. I'm on the boat now. I wave to Carlos,

While the priest finishes his routine prayer.

Old, Latin words surround me; they shield me from the blank, dead city where I am seen.

This time I let Carlos win.

8.

Before. In the run-down apartment that Mireya and Lucinda share, the phone rings. The answering machine plays message (in Mireya's voice) after sixth ring: "This is number twelve B, we're not here, okay? Leave a message..."

Mireya appears with boxes in hand.

MIREYA

Leave a message, dammit.

Answering machine registers random noise followed by silence, then click of phone hang-up.

LUCINDA: *[from other room]* Did you pick up?

MIREYA: No. I want to know who it is. Why don't they leave a fucking message?

LUCINDA: *[enters with duffle bag and clothes]* They're just playing with us.

MIREYA: Well, I don't like it. I don't like this fucking game. If they can't leave a message and at least say who they are, I won't answer the phone and that's that. What are you doing?

You're going somewhere?

LUCINDA: Yes.

MIREYA: To some place with a pool, eh?

LUCINDA: They're keeping Carlos somewhere. I have to find him.

MIREYA: Based on what? Some film this guy shows you. Are you sure it was even Carlos in that film?

LUCINDA: I know my own brother.

MIREYA: We see what we want to see.

LUCINDA: It was Carlos. It was his face, his voice....

MIREYA: You really trust this Claudio, don't you?

LUCINDA: He risked his life for me.

MIREYA: When did this act of heroism take place?

LUCINDA: They beat him up. I found him in the alley outside an old movie theater.

MIREYA: I didn't think there were any movie theaters left.

LUCINDA: He was bleeding. A real mess.

MIREYA: And you helped him, I suppose?

LUCINDA: I helped him up. Yes. Got him cleaned up. Old man in a kiosk gave us some sugar to stop the bleeding. Claudio didn't want me to help him. He said "Go on. Go away."

I think he was ashamed. He didn't want me to see him like that. But I didn't leave until I knew he'd be all right.

MIREYA: ...He could've orchestrated the whole thing. To gain your sympathy.

LUCINDA: You know, for someone who doesn't really like stories, you sure like to make them up.

MIREYA: Who said I don't like stories?

LUCINDA: Not once have you mentioned a single book...

MIREYA: There are all kinds of stories, honey.

LUCINDA: Soaps.

MIREYA: I like my soaps, okay? At least they still broadcast them.

LUCINDA: Two fucking channels.

MIREYA: Better than nothing.

LUCINDA: Damn government.

MIREYA: Our government, remember? We voted them in, in the end. It was democratic.

LUCINDA: Save us all from such democracy.

MIREYA: If your vote didn't get counted...

LUCINDA: It's not your fault or anyone's fault. I know. All blame's gone out the window.

MIREYA: What use is it to blame?

LUCINDA: None. But accountability...yes. It'd be useful if someone was actually accountable for all the shit.

MIREYA: What makes you believe Claudio?

LUCINDA: I trust what he showed me was real.

MIREYA: A fragment of a video... Okay. So, let's say it was real. Let's say Claudio is a heroic piece of shit. What's your plan? Head out, wander about, see if you can find your brother?

LUCINDA: Claudio's putting me in touch with someone. He said she'd help.

MIREYA: Who's this she? If something happens to you, I'll need to know.

LUCINDA: Nothing's going to happen.

MIREYA: You're immune to everything?

LUCINDA: I just have to do this, all right? I can't stay here pretending Carlos is going to come back on his own. I have to...cause if I don't...I'm going to forget him. I'm starting to forget him already. The other day I was walking around the old park where we used to go on Sunday mornings and I couldn't...

I couldn't remember his face. Not a single detail...I have to do this. Whatever happens....I have to....At least I can say I'm doing something, which is more than I can say for you.

MIREYA: You think I'm not doing anything? I got a job. I'm selling potato waves.

LUCINDA: What the hell are potato waves?

MIREYA: *[taking box out of the larger box]* An appliance. You can bake four potatoes in the microwave in three minutes with this thing.

LUCINDA: We don't have a microwave.

MIREYA: But other people do, right?

LUCINDA: Not around here.

MIREYA: It's a job, okay? I'm working. I'm being useful to society. I keep things moving forward.

LUCINDA: You really believe that?

MIREYA: I sell all these boxes, they'll pay me plenty.

LUCINDA: In what? Ration cards?

MIREYA: We can't all be readers, honey.

LUCINDA: ...You think I'm fucking him, don't you?

MIREYA: What you do with Tomás is no business of mine.

LUCINDA: We're paying the rent, aren't we?

MIREYA: But you're going away, aren't you? On your trusty tip from Claudio. How are we going to pay the rent, then?

LUCINDA: It's only for a couple hours, at most a day or two.

MIREYA: Twenty miles becomes two thousand miles and before you know it, they'll have you gone too. ...And what do I do? Let the phone ring, listen to their non-messages...sell potato waves...

LUCINDA: I'll be all right.

MIREYA: What kind of reckless shit...? This is not some story you're living out of one of your beloved books. Christ, can't you see they just want your money? They're making you go through all this shit, raising your fucking hopes, and in the end they're just going to take your money and you'll be done with. On some heap somewhere. Like they've done with so many.

LUCINDA: This is different.

MIREYA: Because it's Claudio? Money's money, Lucinda. Be it Claudio or whomever. Whatever they take from you is going to go straight into putting up more shiny new government buildings or cameras or devices that don't have names yet. But it won't go into finding your brother.

LUCINDA: ...What do you want me to do, then?

MIREYA: I want you to stay here. I want you to be with me. I want to look out at the city, our beautiful city, and not feel ashamed

At what's become of it, and what's becoming of it. Every day another building comes down, every day more people are lost, every day I see the children look at me more and more like a stranger. You don't belong here, their eyes say.

What kind of language do you speak? Who do you pray to? What do you believe in? I want to hit them. Smash their skulls in. I want to become a murderer. This is normal, I tell myself. This is how we live. I want to forget myself. I want to pretend I'm a movie queen

Dancing some silly ethereal strut that everyone decides to imitate. Adoration. Yes. That's what I want. Simple, fascistic adoration so that I can keep pretending the last thread of blood has been forever silenced by shells, even though I know more and more blood will seep into the metal sea. What will become of me? Watching TV, counting my rations, drinking stale tea?

Who will I be in five years time? Ten years time? Twenty? If I'm lucky... What kind of murderer will I be? Casual? Unthinking? Or will I still feel something for my delirious city?

You want completion, a sense of order and peace. There is none. Even if you do find Carlos...There never will be again. (*Slight pause. The phone rings.*)

LUCINDA: I'll answer it.

MIREYA: No. Let it ring. Let them do whatever they like.

The phone keeps ringing.

9.

In Tomás' apartment later the same evening.

TOMÁS: When I was twelve, I re-designed the whole city. I had this amazing plan.

There were going to be waterways and walkways, parks, and rows of intersecting buildings that would open up onto gardens filled with stones and flowers year-round.

Everything would be new, but graced with something old. I didn't want to destroy everything and start over, you see?

To me, the city already had purpose and beauty. I just wanted to illuminate its possibilities. I didn't know anything. I was twelve. I only had dreams of being an architect.

I didn't understand the practicalities of construction, the legalities of zones, or the fiscal compromises that could alter a vision.

To me, it was all just a matter of realizing a drawing, figuring out dimensions and scales, drafting an imagined reality into being. If I'd known then....

LUCINDA: What would become of the city...

TOMÁS: I'd have stopped dreaming.

LUCINDA: ...Fire in the sky.

TOMÁS: Is there?

LUCINDA: Up ahead.

TOMÁS: And after there'll be rain.

LUCINDA: There always is.

TOMÁS: Best not go out.

LUCINDA: We can't all stay in.

TOMÁS: Some of us have a choice, you mean?

LUCINDA: You should rest.

TOMÁS: I'm well-rested.

LUCINDA: I'll close the window.

TOMÁS: Leave it.

LUCINDA: It'll get cold.

TOMÁS: Cold, fire...what difference does it make? You're leaving me.

LUCINDA: It's only for a day or two, Tomás.

TOMÁS: They all say that. They never come back. ...Go to the kitchen. I've some money inside the cereal box. Take it.

LUCINDA: No.

TOMÁS: Take it.

LUCINDA: You're getting upset. It's not good for you.

TOMÁS: You treat me like a child.

LUCINDA: I only want what's best for you.

TOMÁS: Words. Empty words out of a book.

LUCINDA: Stop.

TOMÁS: You want me quiet, eh? Pensive Tomás, sad Tomás, twelve-year-old Tomás dreaming of his precious city...Take the money, Lucinda. I know what these people are like. They always want more.

LUCINDA: I'll be fine.

TOMÁS: That's what I thought, and look what happened...Tomás, well-regarded architect, goes outside the gated zone, the gated community that's supposed to be safe:

free from insurgents, free from violence.

He steps outside the paths he knows and the clandestine byways he frequents on occasion. He wants to see someone, someone from his past. A woman. They tell him – the mysterious "they," the movers and makers who configure and reconfigure all the stories, the "they" we demonize and prophet-ize at one and the same, because they're us, whether we like it or not –

they tell him she's over there in another town

locked away in a safe house, but we can find her; we can get her out of there if you just give us the money. So, Tomás, the well-regarded architect with centrist political views; Tomás, the dutiful son who never saw fit to rock any boat because he just wanted a career, finds himself handing over the money, lots of money, to people he barely knows. He does this out of love. The woman from his past is a former lover, you see? And Tomás does lose himself over love. Everything goes as planned.

Money's exchanged, passage is arranged.

It's a perfect story. He even gets to see the woman. Oh yes. They release her for a few hours just so he can see her, just so that the illusion of emotional restoration can be sustained. Well, Tomás is overjoyed. He can't quite believe it. He's the hero of this story. Money has answered his prayers and even brought him back his love; And then no more than a half hour later, after Tomás and his lover are driving off far along on the road, back toward the gated zone and its promise of safety, the car swerves unexpectedly; it hits something – a rabbit? A dog? – and then an explosion, and Tomás never sees his lover

or anything else ever again. ... *[quoting from memory line from* Great Expectations*]* "It is a most miserable thing to feel ashamed of home...a black ingratitude..." ...Give me your hand. You're trembling.

LUCINDA: I'm not.

TOMÁS: You're afraid.

LUCINDA: I won't be.

TOMÁS: How many times will you say that to yourself to make it true?

LUCINDA: Tomás...

TOMÁS: Too childish for you?

We're never too old for childish things, childish thoughts... *[paraphrasing from line from* Great Expectations*]* It's impossible to separate the past or present from the innermost life of life.

LUCINDA: Are you reading to me?

TOMÁS: From memory. Yes. Does it surprise you? I remember everything; even what's not true: what I imagined once. It's all part of memory now. Don't go, Lucinda. Please. I love you.

LUCINDA: You speak about love. You use that word. You dream of the city. I dream about my twin. He speaks to me in dreams. He reminds me of the promise we made to each other

When we were young, the promise to protect each other always. Simple, really. Except not so simple because when I should have protected him, when I should have fucking been there for him, I wasn't. I was shopping, browsing, lost in myself and things. Stupid things. And I don't even know what I was looking at. Toys? Gadgets? What?

TOMÁS: It's not your fault.

LUCINDA: Dead Carlos, useless Carlos, ghost Carlos...It's all I can think about now. I see his body broken by hands filled with rings; I see his flesh punctured and ripped...He's cut open. I see this. In my mind. His insides are pulled from his body, and sold to someone somewhere across the sea, like they do with so many...*(half-sung)* "For sale, all life is for sale;

This is the lullaby of the good and gone:

For sale." I can't love. I can't move on.

I can't put my brother's name on the list of the dead, and accept the mess we live in because it's all we have. And I won't pretend that I love you just because I need a job.

TOMÁS: ...You should close the window. Go to the kitchen. Take the money. Take it all.

LUCINDA: Tomás...

TOMÁS: Go. Please. Just go.

Lucinda walks away. Tomás sits in silence. It begins to rain.

10.

In an abandoned area of the city, under shelter, Lucinda stands with small duffle bag in hand. Joan, transvestite mercenary, appears.

JOAN: Lose it.

LUCINDA: What?

JOAN: The bag. Come on.

LUCINDA: It's just a

Joan grabs the duffle bag from Lucinda, cuts it open with a knife.

JOAN: Shit. Nothing but shit. What'd you need this for? You think you're going to some party? Huh? Some fancy do? Where's the money? Come on.

LUCINDA: How do I...?

JOAN: I'm here, right? I'm the one you've been waiting for.

LUCINDA: Joan?

JOAN: Yeah.

LUCINDA: You don't look –

JOAN: What do you care? I'm Joan and that's all there is to it, honey.

LUCINDA: Claudio said-

JOAN: No more names, dear. This isn't some chirp-and-chat. You got it?

LUCINDA: Yes.

JOAN: Give. Give. *(Lucinda hands money over; Joan counts)* Fucking joke this. Give the rest.

LUCINDA: I don't –

JOAN: Give it. *(strikes Lucinda)*

LUCINDA: Don't...

JOAN: You're giving orders now? Who the fuck are you? Are you running this show all of a sudden? Now, give or we don't go nowhere. Road ends here, see? Fucking terminus. No traffic, no rush hour. No fucking lights. *(Lucinda hands over more money.)* That's more like...Very nice. Very good. All in order now.

LUCINDA: Are we?

JOAN: Oh yes. Right on track; on business.

Come on. Get in.

LUCINDA: What?

JOAN: Here.

Joan strikes Lucinda unconscious, lifts a grate in the ground and pushes Lucinda into darkness, unseen.

11.

Sudden blinding light. Lucinda is revealed in a stark but oddly chic anteroom, which has the feel of a hotel lobby. She is seated, handcuffed to the chair.

Claudio appears.

CLAUDIO: You're safe now.

LUCINDA: My wrists are bleeding.

CLAUDIO: You shouldn't exaggerate.

LUCINDA: What should I do? Applaud your actions?

CLAUDIO: I've done nothing but help you.

LUCINDA: Is that what you call this?

CLAUDIO: I've located your brother.

LUCINDA: In another movie?

CLAUDIO: He's being transported here.

LUCINDA: ...My head hurts.

CLAUDIO: ...You handed over a great deal of money.

LUCINDA: Enough?

CLAUDIO: Where'd you get it?

LUCINDA: You've been watching me. You must know.

CLAUDIO: You're not my only case, Ms. Caval.

LUCINDA: Such formality...

CLAUDIO: I prefer it that way.

LUCINDA: I thought you'd prefer numbers.

CLAUDIO: Why?

LUCINDA: Less of a loss when you kill me.

CLAUDIO: I don't kill people, Ms. Caval.

LUCINDA: No. You guard old movie theaters.

CLAUDIO: Actually, it's been torn down. We saw the last of it.

LUCINDA: Poor culture.

CLAUDIO: Quite rich, actually.

LUCINDA: You really believe that?

CLAUDIO: Belief, Ms. Caval, faith is crucial to a society's survival.

LUCINDA: To my survival?

CLAUDIO: Nothing's going to happen to you.

LUCINDA: You're going to take care of me?

CLAUDIO: I'll do whatever's required.

LUCINDA: Including getting yourself beat up?

CLAUDIO: ...You were very kind that day.

LUCINDA: And this is how you thank me.

CLAUDIO: If it's any comfort to you, Ms. Caval, it – that day – it wasn't planned.

LUCINDA: It was a random beating, then?

CLAUDIO: Yes. As a matter of fact, it was.

LUCINDA: Poor Claudio.

CLAUDIO: Don't say my name like that. After all I've done for you...

LUCINDA: What have you done?

CLAUDIO: Do you think all this, locating your brother, just happened by God's grace and God's grace alone?

LUCINDA: I'm sorry.

CLAUDIO: Words....Limpid, languid, liquid...(leeched from the soul)...There is greatness, Ms. Caval, the possibility of it rests within us, if we let it.

LUCINDA: Where's my brother, then? Where is he?

CLAUDIO: ...You have to be patient.

LUCINDA: Like her?

CLAUDIO: What?

LUCINDA: Your wife. ...Is this where they kept her?

CLAUDIO: I don't know where she was taken, where she was kept, if she was kept... All I know is she's gone.

LUCINDA: So's Carlos.

CLAUDIO: He's alive. I promise you that much.

LUCINDA: Fuck piss shit motherfucker.

CLAUDIO: Language. The sign. See?

A discreetly embedded electronic scroll that repeatedly reads "#$&%" is revealed on one of the walls of the room.

LUCINDA: This place...smells of death.

CLAUDIO: You know, when I came here, to this hotel, for the first time, I must've been about ten or twelve, I remember thinking who would ever come here? The place was filthy. Truly filthy. The people who brought me here at the time said it'd been a great spa once a long time ago where all the rich came to make themselves feel better. I wanted to see it, you know, in my mind, really imagine it, but I couldn't. All I could think about was how run-down it was, and how every bit of it was dirty, reeking of dirt everywhere, and how impossible it would be to make it right again.

And yet now... well, perhaps it's hard for you to see, because well, you haven't really. You've only seen this room but if you were to see it, if you were to see this entire hotel, you'd be amazed how beautiful it is: Truly restored to what must have been its former glory. Even if it's not a spa anymore. I'm telling you this because, I don't know why. perhaps because all you've seen is the destruction, you know,

The tearing down of things; And I want you to know...This government that perhaps you've feelings against – In fact I know you do... And I promise you you're not here under interrogation. I wouldn't do that to you;

This is purely a contract of sorts, an exchange of money for a person's life – for their finding.

That's what's agreed between us – But this government, well, it does restore, you see?

It's committed to restoration: the putting back together of lost things. I've come to believe that. Over time. Almost in spite of myself.

You see, we're not that different. We're both skeptical, right? That's the word. Not trusting, really. Wary of what's possible, of what could be true. I understand that. I mean, a part of me is still...not sure why my wife... Or even who those men were...phantoms, you know. Ghost palace. That was your phrase. I feel that. Yes. That we're living in a ghost palace of sorts.

But a palace nonetheless. Right? That's what we aspire to. We're all entitled, after all – all of us. That's what democracy means. I want you to understand this because I know you think me somehow condoning of evil, and I want you to know that couldn't be further from the truth of me, of who I am or who I represent. Of course, we all represent the same thing, don't we? That's the truth we live now. And it's exhilarating. Isn't it? To be really free. Don't you feel that?

LUCINDA: Freedom?

CLAUDIO: It's the state we're in. Okay, surveillance. Okay, the guarded areas outside the gated zones of the city. It may not seem like freedom, but it is, you know. And loss is just part of knowing what freedom is. I think ultimately that's why extreme loss is made known to us. So that we can understand freedom and its beauty. Because once we're restored... I mean, if my wife were to suddenly appear to me again... I know it'd be... well, difficult, of course, because there'd be the hurt and the anger and would she still love me again? But even with all that... I think yes...If I could have her back... I'd appreciate this country so much more. I know I'd be a better citizen, which is what we all want to be, isn't it? Are you listening to me?

LUCINDA: Yes.

CLAUDIO: I don't kill people, Lucinda. I want you to know that. Because I feel, well, doubt...

Because you're here, under odd, let's say, circumstances, not entirely of your own volition, part of a strange transaction, I suppose is how you'd see it, but this must be clear, whatever else you may think of this place

And all this time and money turned over,

My life is devoted to freedom, and its restoration. That is all. (*Claudio approaches Lucinda and uncuffs her.*) Come. I'll take you to him. You'll have seven minutes. No more. You can speak to him, but there'll be no touching. Physical contact is prohibited. Understand?

LUCINDA: Yes.

CLAUDIO: After you see him, his exit will be processed, and safe passage will be arranged.

I know you want more time, but just remember you'll have it soon enough. You'll have all the time in the world.

He leads her away.

12.

A bright room with a high ceiling. Part of the room has been partitioned with glass. It is on this side of the room where Carlos is seated. He wears the same clothes as he wore in the video fragment. Lucinda sits opposite.

CARLOS: How much did you pay for me?

LUCINDA: Doesn't matter.

CARLOS: Shouldn't have.

LUCINDA: ...Have they hurt you?

CARLOS: If you're going to cry...

LUCINDA: I won't. I'm sorry...It's just been a long time.

CARLOS: I missed you.

LUCINDA: I'd dream you. Your body would tell me things in dreams. All sorts of signs. I tried to follow them.

CARLOS: I dreamed too.

LUCINDA: Yeah?

CARLOS: When I could... sleep. ...What is it?

LUCINDA: You don't look like yourself.

CARLOS: How should I look?

LUCINDA: I don't know. Taller.

CARLOS: I'm the same, Lucinda. Have you forgotten me already?

LUCINDA: Of course not. It's just...

CARLOS: Long time.

LUCINDA: Yes.

CARLOS: I didn't recognize you at first.

LUCINDA: Do I look that different?

CARLOS: You look scared.

LUCINDA: I'm not.

CARLOS: You were never scared. I remember that about you.

LUCINDA: I'd almost forgotten.

CARLOS: It's good to see you.

LUCINDA: I don't want to know what they've done to you. I don't ever want to know. I've already imagined everything that could possibly be imagined.

CARLOS: Okay.

LUCINDA: Promise.

CARLOS: I promise.

LUCINDA: Like that game we used to play.

CARLOS: What game?

LUCINDA: Our game with words.

CARLOS: I don't know what you're talking about.

LUCINDA: We made it up. When we were little. It was a silly game. We called it the promise game. You'd say a word, then I'd build on it, and then you'd build on mine and then we'd keep topping each other until all we could say to each other was "promise."

CARLOS: Promise.

LUCINDA: Yes.

CARLOS: ...Teach me.

LUCINDA: How could you not remember?

CARLOS: What difference does it make if I remember or not? I'm your brother, right? That's all you should care about. I'm not a terrorist. I'm a good citizen. I always have been.

LUCINDA: I never said-

CARLOS: You don't have to. Nothing but judgment in your eyes cause of some stupid game...

LUCINDA: Carlos...

CARLOS: I don't go by that now.

LUCINDA: What do you go by?

CARLOS: 1-4-5-5.

LUCINDA: Is that your-?

CARLOS: Yeah. I don't like names. They screw things up.

LUCINDA: It was our father's name.

CARLOS: What?

LUCINDA: Carlos Reyes. Don't you remember?

CARLOS: All you want to do is talk about the past. It's got nothing to do with me now.

LUCINDA: When we're back in the city... everything will come back to you.

CARLOS: What makes you think I want to go back?

LUCINDA: You have to.

CARLOS: I don't have to do anything. Who are you to tell me what I have or don't have to do? You were always like that. Ordering me around. Not anymore. I like it here. It's clean.

LUCINDA: You're not yourself.

CARLOS: You have some idea in your head of who I am and who I'm supposed to be. You've never seen me clearly. There was nothing for me in the city. I wanted to leave. I asked them to take me. That day at the mall...I had it all figured out. And you've come all this way to bring me back? You've wasted your time, Lucinda. I'm not going. I'll never leave. And stop that. ...Stop crying.

LUCINDA: What's happened to you?

CARLOS: Nothing. I'm happy.

LUCINDA: Waving to ghosts.

CARLOS: What?

LUCINDA: Like you always said.

CARLOS: I never said that.

LUCINDA: Carlos...

CARLOS: I told you. It's 1-4-5-5. That's what I answer to.

LUCINDA: ...I'll teach you the game. Would you like that?

CARLOS: All right.

LUCINDA: You have such beautiful eyes.

CARLOS: I wish you'd stop crying.

LUCINDA: I wish I could hold your hand.

CARLOS: We could pretend, if you want.

I can hold mine up. You could hold yours. We could almost touch.

LUCINDA: Yes. (*They do so.*) Your hands are so rough.

CARLOS: They've always been like that. You just never noticed.

LUCINDA: I don't know what to believe anymore.

CARLOS: Believe what you want.

LUCINDA: ...That you're my brother.

CARLOS: Yes.

LUCINDA: That you love me.

CARLOS: Yes.

LUCINDA: That we'll be together always. And you'll never leave me.

CARLOS: Yes.

LUCINDA: That this day never happened.

CARLOS: Erased.

LUCINDA: Gone from memory.

Buzzer rings indicating their time together is up.

A door on the partitioned side of the room opens. Carlos exits.

Lucinda remains, her hand held up to where Carlos' palm once was.

13.

In splintered time and multiple views.

MIREYA: The phone rings. It's always ringing.

I've gotten used to it. Let the bastards call all they want. I'm not going to answer. But this time, I don't know... this time I do. They say it's Lucinda.

TOMáS: They say she's been seen. Far away. Outside the main gates of the city. They say she's been in an accident.

CLAUDIO: I tell her to wait. I'm very clear.

But she won't listen. She's gotten it into her mind that she can do things her own way.

She doesn't even know where she is. We're at the far edge of the city. It's rough terrain.

But she keeps on anyway.

MIREYA: She's always been like that. Stubborn, you know. But this time, well... I don't know what to make of it. Because truth is, she doesn't know how to drive. I tell them that. Do you think they listen?

CLAUDIO: It was routine. She gets in a car, and goes off. She keeps insisting Carlos is with her. What am I going to say? If that's what she wants to believe....

MIREYA: She slammed straight into the gates. The car was wrecked. They pulled her out. She was still breathing. Someone called an ambulance. There's still time.

TOMáS: It's been several days now. Still no word. I start to imagine what life will be like without Lucinda reading to me. Her voice fills the room. I can still hear it. A very strange, tender emotion hits me. I leave the window open. I let the cold air in. I imagine lots of fires in the sky, and start drawing Lucinda

in my mind.

CLAUDIO: They remodel the office of records. She won't recognize it. She probably won't like it. No doubt she'll blame me. For everything.

I'll take the blame. After all, I was right next to her in the car. I let her drive.

MIREYA: She gets put in hospital. She falls into a coma. There's no point in waiting anymore. There's nothing I can say. Carlos is dead. She was never going to find him.

TOMáS: I go out. I listen to everyday things.

I don't feel like staying in the apartment anymore. People push me in the street. I'm too slow for them. I let them. I find my way.

The air is crisp. The sun beats. I walk the city the way I did when I was fifteen. It's as if Lucinda is guiding me.

CLAUDIO: I see her at the hospital. It's late.

Everyone's gone. I came because, I don't know... I want to tell her, I want her to know that I did all I could but in the end, in the end, I could only do what I was told: Take the money; make her believe it's him, and make sure she leaves before she sees Carlos is really dead, has been dead for quite some time.

There were bodies buried near the pool. There were bodies underneath the floorboards of the sun room. The place reeked of death. It'll never be clean. ... She waves to me. She's sitting in the hospital bed in a full coma and she waves. Like I'm a ghost.

MIREYA: I hate hospitals. They're too clean.

I tell her, not that she can hear me, but I tell her anyway this is the last time, okay? I'm not coming back here. I go back to the apartment and make some tea. Oo-long. There's a box hidden way back in the cupboard. It has a funny taste. I drink it anyway.

14.

Away from the gray-white room, Lucinda walks down the hospital corridor.

LUCINDA: Nobody can see me. I walk the length of the corridor. Everything's a quiet hum. Carlos is waiting for me at the end of the corridor. He's smiling. He's not angry anymore. I want to tell him I'm all right, not to worry, but he can't hear me. So, I wave. Just like he always does. Stupid childish wave. But I do it anyway. He has a boat. He's made it himself. It's long and narrow with strange, printed sails. He's been working on it for months, he tells me. All this time I've been waiting for him, he's been at work. He wanted to surprise me, he says. The boat's stationed down by the river, as the river winds, twenty miles from the sea. Everything's ready, he says.

He looks so happy.

I look back toward the city edged by black sand and yellow dogs. I look back to see if I can see Tomás sitting by the window in the half-light. I want to see him before we leave.

I want to explain things. I want to tell him I do love, and love deeply. But he's too far away. I can't make him out.

Carlos takes hold of my hand. The boat starts to move. There's a great sense that everything's going to be really clean now. Carlos looks at me. His eyes are clear. He's really happy.

Every inch of the boat is made of books, all the censored books of the world. Carlos has been saving scraps for months. He's scavenged every corner of the city. He's found bits of one novel and parts of another. The books sway in the water. They're bound by thin, rough rope.

The parchment bleeds ink. Soon we are covered in remnants of words. Vowels stain our throats, and illuminate our tongues.

There's nothing but water now and floating words inking our journey. The identity of all things is made raw. For a second I'm back in the hospital. I see Claudio standing in the doorframe. He wants to tell me something,

But I'm gone.

All that's left is the boat of books edging toward the horizon.

End of play

STEAL BACK LIGHT FROM THE VIRTUAL

(after *Theseus* and *Minoutaur*)

by

CARIDAD SVICH

Script History:

This play was developed at the 2009 HotINK International Festival in New York City under Jose Zayas' direction (curator: Catherine Coray), and in earlier versions of the script at Evidence Room and Theater of Note in Los Angeles, and also at New Dramatists in New York City under Anne Kauffman's direction.

It was also presented as a reading (in translation by Jasen Boko) at Zagreb Youth Theatre as part of the 2010 US-Croatia Exchange hosted by Wax Factory/NY, and was a finalist for the 2010 XYZ Festival at About Face Theatre, Chicago, Illinois.

Characters:

TIMOTHY, a man who is unsure in his skin, of where he is or where's been, impulsive and a bit trusting

NADJA, a woman who eats words and steals images through a camera's lens, slightly feral and mindful of her own tenderness,

LAME, a young man who wants to be somewhere he's not, a hustler, immediate in his needs and desires

ANGE, a young woman who eats ice cream and watches movies, exclusively, a runaway, practical and a bit uncentered

MESMER, a journalist with a lighter in his hand, opaque and intelligent

ARIADNE, his wife, who drinks and guards her intimacy, elegant and vengeful

Time & Place:

The present. A labyrinth.

Notes:

This play may be performed with an interval.

Act One

Scene one

A mobile phone rings. The sound of a crash, and car wheels screeching. Si-lence. 4 AM. Cramped square of a space. Graffiti on the walls. Light falls through a slat high up. TIMOTHY and NADJA are seated. He is smoking incessantly. She gnaws on an edible bracelet.

NADJA: I eat words.

TIMOTHY: I smoke shit.

NADJA: My mouth is full. My belly pops. I need more.

TIMOTHY: Have a lie-down.

NADJA: I need to taste them.

TIMOTHY: It's four in the... It's late. My lungs are shot.

NADJA: If you have another smoke...

TIMOTHY: It's this, it's this...I can't even...Everything's shit. Clothes, the newspaper, the tube, value meals the size of a quarter, breakfast that doesn't sit in your stomach for more than a hour and you have to vomit cause the bacon and cheese turns into card-board, speed-dial buttons that don't advance you even a tenth of a second while you hang on the line waiting, investing minutes in nothing, blankets made of some synthetic what's-it that doesn't even warm you, not like when you were a kid and you could curl up into anything for hours and read... who reads? I can't even keep my eyes straight for... fucking virtual orgasms. That's what we have now.

NADJA: Have a word.

TIMOTHY: What?

NADJA: *[offers bracelet]* Come on.

TIMOTHY: What's that?

NADJA: "Bubble."

TIMOTHY: Bubble?

NADJA: It's a good word.

TIMOTHY: It's round.

NADJA: Go on.

TIMOTHY: Don't you want it?

NADJA: I give freely.

TIMOTHY: You spoil me.

NADJA: I'm still capable of love.

TIMOTHY mouths the word "bubble" silently, then eats what's left of her bracelet. Dark.

Scene two

Night. Light barely falls through the slat high up. NADJA watches TIMOTHY sleep. She takes off his red sneakers. She sings to him softly.

"In the Stolen Part"

NADJA: Would you give a toss

if all was lost?

Would you hide away with me?

In the stolen part

of my battered heart

You could be...

Would you let me go

if the world was blown?

Would you still look out for me?

In the stolen part

of my screwed-up heart

You could be...

You could be...

Dark.

Scene three

[Light. Time has passed. The cramped square of space is filled with cigarette butts. We can now see that TIMOTHY's trousers are stained with blood. He is smoking. NADJA is buttoning her blouse.]

TIMOTHY: Give me more.

NADJA: I'm out.

TIMOTHY: You're rotten.

NADJA: I give freely. Just tired now. Need rest.

TIMOTHY: Where the hell...? I can't even move in this place. We're in some... what? A global what's-it?

NADJA: Flat.

TIMOTHY: Fucking two-by...I feel your stink.

NADJA: It's late.

TIMOTHY: Yes. And we've been... fucking

NADJA: All this time.

TIMOTHY: ...I got to get on the autobahn.

NADJA: We're not in Germany.

TIMOTHY: But I thought...

NADJA: Give a think.

Pause.

Do you remember now?

TIMOTHY: I was smoking.

NADJA: You still are.

TIMOTHY: I was looking at you. I was standing outside a building that used to be a TV station.

NADJA: A Teletubbie on your back.

TIMOTHY: My life's possessions inside the belly of a plastic-headed plush creep.

NADJA: Your eyes were tearing.

TIMOTHY: My girl had left me. All the girls leave me.

NADJA: We went inside a club.

TIMOTHY: Inside a church. Your skin was glowing.

NADJA: Under the ultra-violet.

TIMOTHY: We were dancing.

NADJA: Holding hands.

TIMOTHY: Like a couple of kids.

NADJA: Your kisses on me...

TIMOTHY: We were in a car.

NADJA: Do you remember now?

TIMOTHY: After dancing, after everything.

NADJA: We crashed.

TIMOTHY: The windshield fell out.

NADJA: We crawled...

TIMOTHY: Feet and arms...My mobile is ringing.

The sound of a mobile phone ringing outside.

I can hear it. ... You must've carried me. You must've dragged me from the car and carried me on your slim back to this flat, this squat-sit...

NADJA: You're imagining things.

TIMOTHY: That's a hell of a lot, isn't it? A hell of a...

NADJA: Nadja.

TIMOTHY: What?

NADJA: That's my name.

TIMOTHY: It's a Samaritan thing, isn't it? Like in the Bible. A good turn. No-body does that anymore. I don't know of anyone...

NADJA: Thank you.

TIMOTHY: What?

NADJA: You could say "thank you." You could lean on me, rest your head.

TIMOTHY: Yes? Thank you, Nadja.

He leans upon her, rests his head. From outside, the mobile phone rings. Dark.

Scene four

Day. Outside the window. The mobile phone is on the ground. It is ringing. LAME and ANGE look at it.

LAME: You answer it.

ANGE: Ain't mine.

LAME: Can't listen to it... driving me...

ANGE smashes the phone against the pavement.

You didn't have to do that.

ANGE: You said you –

LAME: Won't know who it is now.

ANGE: Wasn't yours anyway.

LAME: It's the principle, isn't it? The principle of the thing.

ANGE: What are you -?

LAME: The phone rings, you pick it up.

ANGE: Where'd you hear that?

LAME: It's a rule.

ANGE: You need to get yourself sorted.

LAME: I'm all right, Ange.

ANGE: You've got everything backwards.

LAME: What do you mean?

ANGE: There are no rules. No principles. Where've you been?

LAME: Blowing cock.

ANGE: You don't know a thing.

LAME: Good money it is.

ANGE: You like it.

LAME: Yeah, but it's still good money.

ANGE: They pay you in Euros.

LAME: Same as dollars.

ANGE: Not the same.

LAME: It is.

ANGE: Where's your math?

LAME: In my head.

ANGE: Lame. That's what you are.

LAME: That's who I am, not what I am. Look, it's just my name.

ANGE: It suits you.

LAME: Fuck off.

ANGE: It does.

LAME: You smashed the fucking mobile. We could've made some money off it.

ANGE: If it was up to you...

LAME: What?

ANGE: Money all the time...

LAME: It's good, isn't it?

ANGE: *[on top of him]* Like cock?

LAME: Don't.

ANGE: Why? Can't I touch it?

LAME: Not here.

ANGE: What's wrong with here?

LAME: It's the street. There are rules, Ange.

ANGE: Yeah?

LAME: The street's one of them.

ANGE: I'll sort you out.

LAME: Don't.

ANGE: You want a mobile? I'll get one for you.

LAME: I don't like the new ones. They've got too many options. There's too much to remember...

ANGE: I'll get you anything you want.

She stays on him.

LAME: You're a cow.

ANGE: Yes.

She goes down on him. Dark.

Scene five

High-rise. Lounge-lush pristine. A wide window that looks onto the city.

MESMER is writing. ARIADNE is drinking.

MESMER: "In this world, in this world there is a proclivity for behavior that doesn't preclude..." Fuck it.

ARIADNE: You were doing fine, Mesmer.

MESMER: I can't write this. I can't write when I don't even believe in what... Look at the street. It's all gray.

ARIADNE: It'll be spring soon.

MESMER: I'm a fraud, Ariadne. A damn two-bit journalist.

ARIADNE: You've won prizes.

MESMER: A complete fraud.

ARIADNE: That's why I'm with you.

Pause.

MESMER: They catch a crime scene on a home camera. It makes the news, and everybody wants their hands on it, don't they? Because it's what?

ARIADNE: Hot.

MESMER: A property. Yes. A car crashes on the road. Two people fly out of a window: a man and a woman. A few seconds later seven young men are killed by a man who is said to have the head of a bull.

ARIADNE: A Minotaur?

MESMER: Yes. And the bodies of the man and woman have disappeared. A camera captures everything.

ARIADNE: Including the Minotaur?

MESMER: His face is unseen, just out of the camera's eye.

ARIADNE: Shame.

MESMER: You'd like to see one?

ARIADNE: It's not every day, is it, that you get to see a man with the head of a bull?

MESMER: True.

ARIADNE: Where did the bodies go?

MESMER: The two people from the car? Perhaps the Minotaur ate them.

ARIADNE: It doesn't work like that.

MESMER: What doesn't?

ARIADNE: Nature.

MESMER: How does it work then?

ARIADNE: The Minotaur sees the woman standing before him and decides to spare her.

He decides she is too beautiful to waste in this world, in this world of men, so he gives her wings, and sends her into the sky so that he can watch her at all times, from wherever he is: the cinema, the phone booth, the hole at the peep show...He can watch her and keep his watch safe over her. He guards her strange beauty.

MESMER: What about the man?

ARIADNE: Which man?

MESMER: There was a man in the car.

ARIADNE: He hid inside the woman's wings.

MESMER: He escaped the Minotaur?

ARIADNE: Yes.

MESMER: He is kind, this beast.

ARIADNE: He understands the meaning of mercy.

MESMER: What about the boys?

ARIADNE: The seven slain?

MESMER: Yes.

ARIADNE: For someone to be saved, there must be a sacrifice.

He kisses her. Dark.

Scene six

The cramped square is wider now. Light fills it in streaks. Time has passed.
TIMOTHY is bent. NADJA is putting on lipstick.

TIMOTHY: It must be morning.

NADJA: It's mid-day. You slept through the night, and another day.

TIMOTHY: The room has changed. This is not the same...you've moved me.

NADJA: This is the same flat. See the graffiti?

TIMOTHY: Blackbirds are singing. There are no blackbirds in Germany.

NADJA: We're not in Germany. I told you before.

TIMOTHY: My mobile has stopped ringing. There are bruises on my legs. What have you done to me?

NADJA: Have a lie-down.

TIMOTHY: You've tricked me.

NADJA: I saved you.

TIMOTHY: I dreamt there was a beast, a strange animal, half-bull...his teeth dug into my flesh. He wouldn't leave me.

NADJA: *[walking away]* Go to sleep.

TIMOTHY: Where are you going? Are you going to leave me like all the other girls?

NADJA: I'll come back.

TIMOTHY: I don't want that beast to...

NADJA: He's only in your dreams.

TIMOTHY: I can't sleep if you're not with me.

NADJA: Timothy. Please.

TIMOTHY: Nadja? Where are we?

NADJA: See the ravens through the window? We're home, love.

TIMOTHY: Do you love me?

NADJA: Be still now.

TIMOTHY: Where are my sneakers?

NADJA: You haven't any.

TIMOTHY: I can't go out without my sneakers. Nadja? Tell me you won't leave me.

NADJA: I won't leave you.

TIMOTHY: Tell me again.

NADJA: I don't have time.

She exits. Dark.

Scene seven

LAME and ANGE stand outside the ice cream shop.

ANGE is eating ice cream in a sugar cone. LAME watches her.

LAME: We could make a killing.

ANGE: Another one of your schemes. I ain't saving you, Lame.

LAME: They're giving out a fucking reward for those dead boys.

ANGE: Who are you going to blame?

LAME: The suit who had me last week.

ANGE: Which one?

LAME: I'll get me a fucking Play-Station, an MP3, one of those nylon mesh jackets with the non-woven fibers, a frock of the week. I could be rich.

ANGE: I don't get a frock?

LAME: Only if you're with me.

ANGE: I want an Alexander McQueen.

LAME: I want a leather number slit up the front with a tight bodice.

ANGE: You're dreaming.

LAME: You don't think I look it?

ANGE: You'd need black kohl eyeliner, glitter varnish, get yourself fixed up.

LAME: I could do it. I could be a damn rock n' roller.

ANGE: Yeah?

LAME: Like Bowie.

Lame sings from chorus of Bowie's "Young Americans." Ange listens, then...

ANGE: Who'd fuck you then?

LAME: Upper class twits.

ANGE: In your dreams.

LAME: ...That suit burned me, all right?

ANGE: So you'll blame him for the killings?

LAME: He burned a hole on my tit. See?

ANGE: Cigarette?

LAME: Fucking bastard.

ANGE: Poor Lame.

LAME: Shut up. He had me cuffed. Fetish queen, but married. He had his ring on. I could see. He runs his forefinger on it to prove to himself what he's doing with me is nothing.

I don't mind except he starts flicking his Zippo too close, with his damn filtered cigarette, in his hand, and I think "What's he...?" He burns me. Right on my tit. Takes the lit cig straight into my skin. And he's smiling. I can't even rub salve on it. It hurts too much. Hole in my fucking chest. Who the hell does he think he is? Leaves me cuffed to the damn bed and he walks out with his Paul Smith trousers and Gucci cufflinks. Click, click. I'm lying there with damn smoke cresting my skin. I can't even scream. He comes back in an hour and un-cuffs me. He had ink on his fingers.

ANGE: Ink?

LAME: Like from a pen.

ANGE: A goddamn writer?

LAME: I don't know. I blew him for a hundred.

ANGE: Whore.

LAME: I was scared.

ANGE: Liar.

LAME: It's the truth, Ange. I swear.

ANGE: What was his name?

LAME: Mesmer.

ANGE: You're making it up.

LAME: He wants to see me again.

ANGE: What kind of name is that?

LAME: God of sleep.

ANGE: What?

LAME: That's what he said. Comes from the God of sleep. From the Greek.

ANGE: That's Hypnos.

LAME: Yeah?

ANGE: Hypnos is the God of Sleep.

LAME: What's Mesmer then?

ANGE: Fucking twit.

LAME: ...Gave me his number. Said I should call him again. He's got nerve, right?

ANGE: So, you're thinking you go to the cops and say this Mesmer, this twit who burned a hole in your tit, killed seven boys off the highway?

LAME: That's right. Seek my reward.

ANGE: Rotten scheme.

LAME: He's fucking scared of his wife. He'd do anything for her not to know about me.

ANGE: *[offers ice cream]* I'm full. You want?

LAME: Give here. *[He licks.]* Got nuts in it.

ANGE: It's pistachio. You don't want it?

LAME: It's all right.

ANGE: The way you eat...

LAME: What?

ANGE: Like a damn girl.

LAME: Quit.

ANGE: You're worse than me.

LAME: Fuck it.

He tosses ice cream.

ANGE: Didn't have to do that.

LAME: I don't like pistachio. It's warped.

ANGE: There's nothing warped about pistachio.

LAME: So, what'd you think?

ANGE: Your scheme? I think it's shit.

LAME: Yeah?

ANGE: I like it.

Lights fade.

Scene eight

High-rise. MESMER is standing.

A Zippo lighter in hand. ARIADNE is seated, half-seen.

MESMER: I don't always burn them. It's not something I do. I'm a quiet man. My wife Ariadne knows this. I abhor violence.

But certain boys? I want to burn them. This boy on whom I was particularly keen... he called me last night. He's looking for me. Will let me do it again, he said. On his other tit. In his armpits. On the backs of his knees. He is offering himself to me on the phone. Who does he think he is? I'll see him tonight. Same hotel. Off a side street. He says he wants a frock: leather with a slit up the front and a tight bodice. Off the shoulder. Exposed. He mentions a shop. Designer boutique. "It's in the window," he says. "It's a girl's frock, but it will fit me." My wife looks at me. She asks me again about the boys who were killed.

Have I written the complete story yet?

They have tracked down the person who shot the crime scene, the person who saw everything. It's a woman. I tell my wife that she is lying. Who would put a camera on her lover going through a window, on seven boys cut open with a knife? What kind of woman would be spared by a minotaur? My wife smiles. I want to meet this woman. I want to burn her skin.

The flick of the Zippo. Dark.

Scene nine

The cramped square of space. The window is now even higher. TIMOTHY reaches for it. He jumps. Higher and higher. Silence.

A mobile phone crashes through the window. TIMOTHY picks it up. He goes to dial. The mobile starts ringing. It won't stop. TIMOTHY looks at it. TIMOTHY smashes the mobile phone. Dark.

Scene ten

Hotel lobby. Stale quiet, potted plants, wet drinks. ARIADNE is seated, an unlit cigarette in hand. LAME enters.

ARIADNE: Light?

LAME: What?

ARIADNE: Have you a light?

LAME: Yeah.

ARIADNE: You look like you smoke. I wouldn't ask otherwise.

LAME: I smoke. Yeah.

ARIADNE: Not filters, though.

LAME: Screw that. I like it strong.

ARIADNE: American cigarettes.

LAME: Yeah. Camels, Marlboros... If I'm going to smoke, I might as well do it right.

He lights her cigarette.

ARIADNE: Thanks.

LAME: Waiting for someone?

ARIADNE: Hmm?

LAME: A guest?

ARIADNE: I like hotels. I like sitting in lobbies. I'm not waiting for anyone. You?

LAME: Might be.

ARIADNE: You don't know?

LAME: I can come back another time.

ARIADNE: Stay.

LAME: Yeah?

ARIADNE: I like you.

LAME: That's a line, isn't it?

ARIADNE: Everything's a line. My husband specializes in them. He's a journalist.

He stages crime scenes so he can write about them as if they were real. That way he gets the exclusive, right? On his own damn story.

LAME: He does that?

ARIADNE: All the time. Wins prizes, the lot. He's a regular star.

LAME: You're proud of him?

ARIADNE: Wouldn't you be?

LAME: He's a liar.

ARIADNE: We're all liars. Just a bit. You're going to tell me you're through and through?

LAME: Well, I...

ARIADNE: You see? We're all the same. Drink?

LAME: What?

ARIADNE: Want a drink?

LAME: I shouldn't.

ARIADNE: Why not?

LAME: I'm waiting for someone. It wouldn't be right if I was all...

ARIADNE: You don't look the type.

LAME: What'd you mean?

ARIADNE: Like you'd have any sort of morality.

LAME: I believe in things.

ARIADNE: I've stopped believing.

When I was a girl, I believed in the Trinity, in faith, in the vespers, and the lighting of candles. I believed that if you prayed, good things would happen in the world, that there would be answers. Simple. Yes. But I believed it. But then one girl in my class got killed, and then another, and I couldn't do anything, no matter how much I prayed. The Trinity couldn't save me. Couldn't save those girls.

I stopped praying. I stopped lighting candles and bowing my head. I stopped waiting for a man to be good to me. And I met my husband. A man with infinite qualities, none of them particularly good, except that he does take care of me. He pays for my upkeep. You see? The nails must be manicured, the hair must be done, the clothes must be...I look good, don't I?

LAME: Yeah.

ARIADNE: You don't mean it.

LAME: I do.

ARIADNE: Don't lie to me. I don't need lies.

LAME: You look a mess.

ARIADNE: That's better. A mess...

LAME: I could fix that.

ARIADNE: With your cock?

LAME: I didn't mean...

ARIADNE: Yes, you did. It's all right. I don't want you. You see? I don't want anybody. I only want my husband. And he despises me.

LAME: You're waiting for him?

ARIADNE: I found a matchbook in his pocket with the name of this hotel. Classic. I know. I'm a cliché. The wronged wife sitting in a hotel lobby with an empty matchbook in her purse, hoping to find her husband, hoping to see the woman he's screwing tonight. I don't wish to confront him. I just want to see what she's like. I want to study her.

LAME: Tips?

ARIADNE: What?

LAME: You want to get tips from her?

ARIADNE: I don't need tips. I know what to wear. I know what looks good on me. I know my worth. No. I just want to see. I want to see how he behaves with her. Does he caress her neck?

Does he slip his hand inside her pants, down her crack, like he does to me? Does he wear the same cologne, the one I got him in Spain for his birthday? Or does he wear something cheap so as to be disguised? Does he want her the same way he wants me?

LAME: I should leave.

ARIADNE: Are you tired of waiting?

LAME: I think I got the wrong night.

ARIADNE: Stay with me.

LAME: I can't. It's not right.

ARIADNE: Such a principled man. I bet you wouldn't resort to killing.

LAME: What?

ARIADNE: Cutting boys open with a knife, sweet adolescent boys with eager faces...

You're not the kind to do such a thing.

LAME: I don't know what you're talking about.

ARIADNE: The news. The boys who were killed. The seven slain.

LAME: Right.

ARIADNE: They show their faces every day at six and eleven. I see them in my sleep. My husband says I am willing them into me, into my dreams. Do you think that's possible? Do you think you can will someone into your sleep?

LAME: I wouldn't know.

ARIADNE: You have such a kind face.

LAME: I should leave.

ARIADNE: Have a drink. Stay with me. I'll caress your skin. I'll give you whatever you need.

She offers him money.

LAME: Don't.

ARIADNE: Am I doing this wrong? Teach me.

LAME: Not here. We'll go up. Yeah?

ARIADNE: Of course. A room.

LAME: Yeah.

ARIADNE: You like hotel rooms, love?

LAME: They're quiet.

ARIADNE: We could all do with a bit of that, eh?

LAME: Finish your drink.

ARIADNE: Will you hurt me?

LAME: I need to think.

She downs the glass. Lights fade.

Scene eleven

The cramped square of space, which is wider now.

TIMOTHY is seated. NADJA walks in with a bag.

TIMOTHY: You came back.

NADJA: I keep my word.

TIMOTHY: I didn't think you would.

NADJA: Eat your fritters.

TIMOTHY: Did you miss me? Did you think about me waiting for you? Did you dream about me?

NADJA: I got us money.

TIMOTHY: Where?

NADJA: Man with a coat.

TIMOTHY: He gave it?

NADJA: We bargained.

TIMOTHY: How much?

NADJA: The price of flesh.

Pause.

TIMOTHY: The fritters are cold. Where'd you get them?

NADJA: Day trip.

TIMOTHY: What? The man in the coat gave you a ticket? An excursion pass?

NADJA: He wanted a ride.

TIMOTHY: I hope he paid you plenty.

NADJA: We rode all the way up to Aberdeen.

TIMOTHY: Aberdeen?

NADJA: Up north a bit. The train was empty, except for some kids on their mobiles calling home. They were sweet. They were calling their parents, tugging at their sneakers and sipping from concealed bottles of Becks. They were talking about football and their favorite teams, ticking away minutes on their mobiles for a bit of home. We sat in the back facing the wrong way.

TIMOTHY: The wrong way?

NADJA: We sat in the opposite direction of where the train was heading.

TIMOTHY: How could you stand it? I always get a headache when I do that.

NADJA: It's what he wanted. He was paying. The kids talked and he ran his hand for a while. Just rubbing. I wanted him to open me but he wouldn't. He said "Not until we are further north and it's all gray."

TIMOTHY: You shouldn't have had to do it.

NADJA: I got us money, didn't I?

TIMOTHY: Cold fritters in my mouth.

NADJA: You need something in you. You can't go out like that.

TIMOTHY: I can't go out at all. You lock the door.

NADJA: I saved you.

TIMOTHY: You picked me up on the street, but I looked out for you, didn't I?

NADJA: I don't need it.

TIMOTHY: I don't even remember what air feels like on my skin. You shut everything out.

NADJA: It's safe here.

TIMOTHY: Damn squat-sit. Everything's ash. Did he screw you?

NADJA: He pushed me down onto the seat of the train as we closed in on Aberdeen and I could see the gray buildings come into view.

Then he pulled the cigarette from his mouth and started burning me. I think he expected me to give him a good cry, but I wouldn't. So he burned me more. All down my belly. See? It was a day trip. He wanted a look at me. A good look. That's what I gave him.

TIMOTHY: He didn't screw you?

NADJA: He left me lying on the seat until the train stopped. Then he said "Let's go for some fritters." I said "Sure, I love fritters. My father used to make them on Saturdays before he'd go drinking."

TIMOTHY: Did he?

NADJA: I lied. I was hungry. He walked me over to a stand and ordered a couple of bags.

Then we sat on the edge of a row of concrete blocks, and ate silently. Like old people do.

Old married couples who sit in parks watching the birds shit as they eat with salty hands.

TIMOTHY: What was he like?

NADJA: Polite. Nice cufflinks.

TIMOTHY: You met him before?

NADJA: No.

TIMOTHY: *[at end of bag]* What's this?

NADJA: A treat.

TIMOTHY: Tastes sweet.

NADJA: Mars bar. Thought you'd like it.

TIMOTHY: It's warm.

NADJA: I got it on the way back. It's fried. Do you like it?

TIMOTHY: I can't think about you with that man...with your stomach all....

NADJA: Shh. Be still.

TIMOTHY: I'm falling asleep. I can't remember anything, Nadja. Something about dancing and a car and going through glass...

NADJA: You'll be fine, love.

TIMOTHY: Do you love me?

NADJA: Be still now.

TIMOTHY: Your voice sounds strange, like it's far away, somewhere else. Where are you from, Nadja?

NADJA: I'm from right here.

TIMOTHY : I can't make you out. I can't find my sneakers. I don't think these clothes are mine. They've been put on me by someone else. I can't find anything, not even my back-pack...

NADJA: You tossed it.

TIMOTHY: Why would I do that, Nadja? Why would I toss my Teletubbie?

NADJA: He was a creep.

TIMOTHY: Did I say that?

NADJA: I'll buy you another.

TIMOTHY: No. It's just I ... I need a cigarette. My brain's mush. I think I must've killed someone. I keep seeing these boys' faces. Their bodies lie off the side of a road. They stare at me. They've got blood in their hair. I don't know where they're from. They look like me when I was seventeen.

NADJA: Have a word.

TIMOTHY: I'm full. My stomach's turning.

NADJA: *[offering the word]* Aberdeen.

TIMOTHY: Aberdeen?

NADJA: Slow doon.

TIMOTHY: What kind of language is that?

NADJA: Just take the words, love.

TIMOTHY: Do you love me?

NADJA: Slow doon.

TIMOTHY: ...Slow doon.

NADJA: Ah go tae bed.

He closes his eyes. NADJA touches her stomach, weeps. Light disappears from the window.

Scene twelve

Hotel room. MESMER is on the mobile phone. This is a close-up.

MESMER: She had the camera tight on me. She wanted to X-ray my eyes, she said. "It's the flicker effect." I looked straight ahead on the train. She had the kind of voice I imagined: a trace of everywhere. She said she'd been to Mexico and that's where she learned to shoot crime scenes. They happen all the time down there, she said. Somebody has to record them.

So, she got into the habit of carrying her camera everywhere.

"I have seven hundred stacks of film. Murders, kidnappings, virtual suicides, sexual coercion, dead boys, girls...I have everything. I'll sell them to you for the right price. I'll sell anything." She has warm eyes. I could lose myself in her. But I keep my gaze. Straight ahead. She places her hand in between my thighs. She starts rubbing. I will not be aroused. I will not let her...She keeps rubbing. Her fingers are insistent. She has practice. I think of her in flames. I think of the man with the head of a bull who haunts me. I will not give in. The train pulls to a stop. We are in a town whose name I cannot pronounce. She says "Mesmer, Mesmer..." How is it she knows my name? I squeeze her hand. I break her fingers. I feel the snap. She will not win.

Lights reveal LAME at MESMER's knees finished with a blow-job. He wears the leather dress with the tight bodice, and black kohl eyeliner. Lights fade.

Scene thirteen

NADJA watches TIMOTHY in the near distance. She dreams in real time.

NADJA: I wake up in London. I go to bed in New York. Glasgow is at the other end of the train, at the other end of Aberdeen, and the northern country:

Caledonia. Los Angeles is the layover of a layover that never ends. Mexico finds me in sleep. Berlin... Berlin steals my dreams. Voices call out on invisible speakers in languages I cannot understand:

"Aspekten der Hypnose, Aspekten der Hypnose..."

This is the suitcase of never ending cities that merge in my brain. Everything is the same.

We are on a piece of cardboard. Points equidistant from each other. The infant universe is flat. Draw a line from one city to the other. Aberdeen lies near Seattle.

The seven slain boys haunt me.

"Aspekten der... *slow doon...*"

Words from one country fall into the other.

I see Timothy leaving. Walk on, boy. Lose me.

There is a glitter on my eyelash from where you kissed me last, from when you were leaning on my cheek. I am an atlas that questions itself daily.

[sings] "Would you give a toss

if all was lost?

Would you still look out for me?"

in the near distance, TIMOTHY is seen crawling out of the window high up of the square space. Dark.

Scene fourteen

Morning. Outside the window.

TIMOTHY is standing. ANGE is thrown onto the street.

ANGE: Damn restaurant prick. All I wanted was an ice cream.

TIMOTHY: Is that all you eat?

ANGE: What?

TIMOTHY: I've seen you through the window. You're always with a cone in hand.

ANGE: Who are you?

TIMOTHY: Timothy.

ANGE: You look a wreck.

TIMOTHY: I feel all right, actually. Just my legs sometimes...hurt... did he hit you?

ANGE: What?

TIMOTHY: The man in the restaurant.

ANGE: Damn prick threw me out. Didn't want a fucking what's-it in his establishment. Socialist pig.

TIMOTHY: What are you to him?

ANGE: Eh?

TIMOTHY: What kind of what's-it?

ANGE: I muck about. I steal things.

TIMOTHY: You're a...

ANGE: A pisser, rotter, spoiler, a spoil on the earth.

TIMOTHY: A junkie.

ANGE: I don't use. Haven't in years. Where are you from?

TIMOTHY: I don't know.

ANGE: Eh?

TIMOTHY: Cities keep changing on me. I thought I was in Berlin for a moment.

ANGE: That's far, isn't it?

TIMOTHY: But then I woke up and I could've sworn I was in London, right? There were ravens outside the window, blackbirds singing, foxes all around. But then I had these fritters, these ice cold banana fritters that tasted like nothing, and I thought I was in Aberdeen, that a part of my body was walking the concrete,

and then I looked at my lover, this woman who found me, and I thought, I'm in New York, right? I'm in goddamn Manhattan in a walk-up on 10th Street or somewhere on a hundred and eleventh, but she looks at me and I see in her eyes that we're in Mexico or maybe it's Los Angeles. I've never been to Los Angeles but her eyes look like L.A. must look, and she says she doesn't know what I'm talking about.

She's half-Russian and her father is from goddamn Paris, and she doesn't remember speaking French as a child, but she does have a vague memory of Berlin, and I think "Right. That's where we are, that's the city I'm in." But she shakes her head and says "No." She says "Look out the window. You'll see where we are." But all I see out the window are feet, a boy with Cherry Docs and jeans, and you holding an ice cream. Pistachio, I believe. And I think "This is a damn labyrinth. There's not even a map for me to figure this out." And this woman who's become my lover who saved me from a car crash I don't even remember, except all I do remember is glass breaking, she says "Look again." And I think "Okay. We're in Toronto. That's where we are. We're in a northern place where everyplace you've been burns into the pavement and tricks your eyes." But she smiles again, and shakes her head, and says "Go to sleep, Timothy. You need a good long rest before you can see where you are."

And my head falls and my dreams turn, and I watch myself crawl out of the window that I couldn't reach... The window that seemed heavy is light as feathers, and I crawl out with ease. I see that my eyes have been shattered by a windshield, which is why I can't make things out. I have been through a crash, you see?

If I hadn't been pulled out by this woman whose eyes look like L.A or some other place I've never been, I'd still be in a car stranded on a road with a wad of money in my backpack. I wouldn't be here looking at you with your bruised eyes hurt by a man you don't even know who wears a suit and tie and works in a restaurant to make ends meet. I'd be lost and more than a little confused. But as I'm here, looking at you, I'm fine. I know everything is a labyrinth, and that's all right.

ANGE: ...You buy me an ice cream?

TIMOTHY: What?

ANGE: There's a place on the corner. Double-dip...

TIMOTHY: I could do anything.

ANGE: The name's Ange.

TIMOTHY: What?

ANGE: That's my name.

TIMOTHY: Ange? That short for something?

ANGE: Let's get an ice cream.

Lights fade.

Scene fifteen

High-rise. Evening. ARIADNE is sitting. MESMER walks in.

ARIADNE: You're late.

MESMER: The city is a bitch.

ARIADNE: That's a strange way of putting it.

MESMER: What do you mean?

ARIADNE: Doesn't sound like you, Mesmer.

MESMER: What? You've never heard me use the word "bitch?"

ARIADNE: You sounded so young for a second.

MESMER: I am young.

ARIADNE: You're not twenty.

MESMER: Neither are you. Are you, dear?

ARIADNE: ...How much work was there?

MESMER: What?

ARIADNE: You're late.

MESMER: I'm always working. Curse of the writer.

ARIADNE: You didn't call.

MESMER: Stop.

ARIADNE: What?

MESMER: You're playing "the wife." Stop it.

ARIADNE: I am your wife.

Pause.

I go to hotels. I sit in a different lobby every night surrounded by plants, soft chairs, cold drinks. It's amazing what you see in a lobby, if you look.

MESMER: I'm glad you're entertained.

ARIADNE: Do you think I'm completely stupid? I could shoot you. I could slay you, let you fall into a ditch like the murderer did with those boys. I'm capable of anything.

MESMER: Have they caught him yet?

ARIADNE: You screwed him, didn't you?

MESMER: Who?

ARIADNE: That boy. The one with the smile, with the distracted smile.

MESMER: I don't screw boys.

ARIADNE: He's a tart. He'll do anyone for money.

MESMER: Have you met someone? Is this what this is about?

ARIADNE: He showed me his tit.

MESMER: He only has one?

ARIADNE: I could shoot you. *[reveals gun]*

MESMER: What are you doing?

ARIADNE: Lame. That's his name, right? Your wretched tart.

MESMER: He's not wretched.

ARIADNE: I married you. I trusted you.

MESMER: Put that gun away.

ARIADNE: I let you humiliate me every night. And you still... with a fucking boy... Pig.

MESMER: Listen to me.

ARIADNE: Pig, pig, pig...

MESMER: Nothing means anything, you see? It's sport, a game, a test of living. I'm not even there. I don't even screw them. I try, but I can't. I won't let myself. Because I love you, you see? I love you too much.

ARIADNE: Pig.

MESMER: I walk down one street. I walk down another. I memorize directions. Nothing means anything. We're a trans-global accident passing each other, going through each other,

through vaginas and cocks...furious, rapid, not knowing what... Seven boys are killed, thrown into a ditch, sacrificed for the well-being of this city, so that people can become concerned, feel connected for a second, so that they are distracted momentarily from their petty lives, but it doesn't mean anything. The boys are dead. A minotaur walks the streets. Someone else will be sacrificed. Our accident, this accident we live in, is a dream. We go from city to city pretending we're the same, pretending everything is all right, but we're substituting real feeling for something else: virtual pleasure, virtual pain. I can't even walk into the office without thinking about your eyes, your body waiting for me at night. My dear Ariadne...And on the other side of the city,

the boy with the distracted smile and the slender waist, and the delicate earring waits...You see? I can't think of anything. So I walk the streets until it is too late, and you are angry from waiting, and you want to kill me with a gun that has sat in a drawer for too long. And I'm even willing to accept killing, to accept death, because it would be something, wouldn't it? It'd be real feeling. Not some...You see? I'm nothing. I can't even walk into our apartment without shaking. The minotaur enters my sleep and I let him devour me, because I know whatever I do, however much I try, I won't love you enough. I'll never save you. And that's what you want, isn't it? You want to be saved. You want the promise of religion. You want ecstasy and beauty and some kind of transcendence. And what do you get instead? You get a butcher boy, a freak, a man with eyes that spin in a trance who cannot, who...

MESMER falls in a fit.

ARIADNE: Mesmer?

The fit continues. ARIADNE sets the gun down. Lights fade.

Act Two

Scene sixteen

Outside the ice cream shop, LAME and ANGE stand. It is cold.

LAME: A fucking brain scan.

ANGE: What?

LAME: He's in the damn hospital.

ANGE: Some scheme...

LAME: It's got nothing to do with that. He's ill or something.

ANGE: Sick?

LAME: Yeah.

ANGE: Did he pay you?

LAME: What's it to you? You've got a new outfit.

ANGE: I met a guy. Fucking loon.

LAME: You screw him?

ANGE: We eat ice cream. He takes me out.

LAME: Day trips?

ANGE: We go to the movies

LAME: ...I've got to see him.

ANGE: Who?

LAME: Mesmer.

ANGE: You're stuck, aren't you?

LAME: Am not.

ANGE: He bought you the frock and everything.

LAME: Looks good on me.

ANGE: Yeah. It does.

LAME: Shiny black lipstick.

ANGE: Is that what you wore it with?

LAME: Yeah.

ANGE: Goddamn coven.

LAME: Nothing like that.

ANGE: You're turning into a fetish queen.

LAME: I like the way it looks. That's all.

ANGE: What? Rock n' roller?

LAME: Yeah.

He sings chorus from Bowie's "Heroes." Ange listens, then...

ANGE: ...You've got to see him.

LAME: I hate hospitals.

ANGE: You've got to sit by his bed. Watch him.

LAME: His wife will be there. She won't like it.

ANGE: You screw her?

LAME: She wanted to try me. I let her.

ANGE: You're a moo, you are.

LAME: She had a sad look.

ANGE: If you don't go to that hospital, he'll die.

LAME: Ain't that serious.

ANGE: Brain scan? That's mortal.

LAME: He's got some kind of disease.

ANGE: You should be ashamed of yourself.

LAME: I didn't know.

ANGE: He rub your tit?

LAME: It's better.

ANGE: Healed, has it?

LAME: Still hurts a bit, but...

ANGE: Your poor sorry heart has decided it's better to have a flaming tit than lose Mesmer's love, is that it?

LAME: Oink.

ANGE: At least I admit it.

LAME: Going to the movies, eating ice cream... going out with a school-boy.

ANGE: He's all right.

LAME: He's probably a fucking murderer.

ANGE: Hey.

LAME: That's what they're like, the worst ones. They come on all nice and then they stab you fifteen times.

ANGE: Fuck off.

LAME: I'm only trying to warn you.

ANGE: You're a fucking cow. A goddamn moo. Go on. Go to your sick boy-friend. Bring him wildflowers.

LAME: He's not my boyfriend.

ANGE: What is he then?

LAME: ...He's Mesmer.

ANGE: Cow.

She walks away.

LAME: Where are you going?

ANGE: To the movies.

Lights fade.

Scene seventeen

NADJA turns her gaze onto the street.

In the background, the flicker of a film.

NADJA: Under the duvet, I dream of Caledonia way up north, I dream of Catalan boys and street singers, scabs on twins in the middle of a square, a black sleeveless T on a body, and an ambient muse. That's what I see, what I listen to, as I turn on my camera and dream.

Timothy's left me. He's stolen away. He's looking for another dream. He's looking out for me. Even though I don't need it. I don't need anything. I've got money, cold fritters, and a bag of chips. I've got chocolate, too. Kit-Kat bars in my pocket in case he comes back to me. I know he likes sweets. Not all the time. But to have...to stick between his teeth.

It's raining smoke. The shops are closed and I turn the other way. Past another street. There's another boy with a bottle of Becks in his hand

and a bouquet of wildflowers. He doesn't know where he is. He doesn't see me. He's got a distracted smile and a hint of contempt on his lips. I'd like to have him under a little tartan blanket, put mirrors on his nipples, so he can reflect everything. I want to make everything private in my life public, including my love, even though it's misplaced, displaced, gone from view. I don't care. Love is a labyrinth. It doesn't know silence. It questions everything.

There is a voice on the loudspeaker. All flights have been cancelled. Barcelona will have to wait for another day, so will Caledonia, and everywhere else on this cardboard map.

I'm on the lip: a place of landing where all facades are dropped. My suitcase holds the future as I stand across from a midnight car park "Get out and don't come back," are the words I hear as I weep alone under the glow of the TV aerials in the dark.

Lights fade.

Scene eighteen

Hospital. MESMER is in bed.

LAME stands before him with a bouquet of wildflowers in hand.

LAME: I brought you these. I thought you'd like them. Wildflowers... I didn't know what else to get. You look so pale lying there. So fragile. I don't think I'd recognize you. You've got such blonde eyebrows. I never noticed that. What do you do, eh? Do you dye them? I'd dye mine but they're so thin, there's no point.

My hair would fall out. I got you wildflowers for luck. They say they're lucky. That's what the woman in the shop said. Cost me a fiver.

You think she stiffed me? I didn't know what to get.

I hate hospitals. Last time I was in one... was when my uncle got cut up. They cut off his leg. It was rotted from the inside. Cancer... I couldn't look at him. I couldn't stay in the room. I can't even walk by hospitals without getting the shivers. Always feel like taking a piss, a real piss, you know what I mean?

You've got a soft mouth. I don't think I noticed that. I always think of you in the dark.

But it's so light here. You can see everything. Can't you? Why do they make hospitals so light? It's not like anyone wants to see how sick they are. Fucking cruel it is. What? You're laughing? It looks like you're smiling. Like you're going to laugh.

I didn't want to see you. I didn't want to come near you. Ange told me to come. She made me. You'd like her. She's not afraid of anything. She picked out my frock, the one you got me. She teased me about it, but she picked it out. I was going to wear it, but I didn't think they'd let me in. It's enough I'm some pug off the street, right?

They said they're testing your brain. Something to do with your fit...I don't know what any of it... I don't even know how they can get into your brain. What are they going to find? I'm having that dream, the one you told me about, the one about the man with the head of an animal. I dream he's eating me, biting off my toes, then my fingers, nipples, earlobes...the delicate parts first, then everything else.

Like those boys on the news, they had their fingers bitten off, did you know that? They said it in one of the papers, one of the ones you're not supposed to believe. But I believe it, because it's in my dream, in the dream you gave me by telling it to me. Some man with the face of an animal bit the fingers off of those boys after they were killed. In my dream, I see your eyes in the face of that animal, and I have to hide under the duvet or else I will scream. I don't even know why I'm here. You've fucking poisoned me. I feel you in my flesh, and every part of me hurts. I was going to seek a reward, some kind of scheme, but fuck that, fuck everything.

They say you're ill, the nurses...They say your brain doesn't work right. Something happened during your seizure. Oxygen left and some part of you stopped. I brought you wildflowers. I thought you'd like them.

They'll make you think of the country, eh? Foxes and trees... But there's no water for them. There's no vase. They're starting to stink.

Lights fade.

Scene nineteen

Outside the cinema, TIMOTHY and ANGE look away from each other.

ANGE: That was a crappy movie.

TIMOTHY: Sorry.

ANGE: Why'd you take me to it?

TIMOTHY: I didn't know what was playing.

ANGE: You could've told me it wasn't a slasher. Would've saved your dime. I only see slashers. They're the only kind of movies I like.

TIMOTHY: Why?

ANGE: Everything else is boring. You feel all right?

TIMOTHY: I think so.

ANGE: You're getting your eyes back?

TIMOTHY: Yes. I'm starting to focus better.

ANGE: What was it like?

TIMOTHY: What?

ANGE: Going through glass?

TIMOTHY: I don't know.

ANGE: Was there blood everywhere? Were any of your bones sticking out? They say you can go up to 10,000 feet if you've got enough oxygen in you. Like you're flying, right? Only without wings.

TIMOTHY: I don't want to talk about it.

ANGE: It helps to forget?

TIMOTHY: Yes.

ANGE: It's all a lie.

TIMOTHY: Sorry?

ANGE: Forgetting. It's a lie. Nobody forgets anything. We just pretend we do.

TIMOTHY: I don't mind.

ANGE: You're a coward.

TIMOTHY: Is this what you're going to be like?

ANGE: What?

TIMOTHY: I took you to a movie. I bought you ice cream.

ANGE: I'm not a schoolgirl, am I?

TIMOTHY: I'm trying to be nice.

ANGE: Why?

TIMOTHY: I don't think I was before.

ANGE: ...Got amnesia, is that it?

TIMOTHY: Of a kind.

ANGE: Like a sci-fi?

TIMOTHY: Yeah.

ANGE: You're my real live sci-fi. I like slasher sci-fis. You ever seen those? People get killed with strange objects.

TIMOTHY: ...Kiss me.

ANGE: What for?

TIMOTHY: I want you to.

ANGE: Buy me a gelato.

TIMOTHY: That's Italian, isn't it?

ANGE: So?

TIMOTHY: There's not an Italian place around here.

ANGE: Look for one.

TIMOTHY: Kiss...

ANGE: No.

TIMOTHY: What's wrong?

ANGE: I don't want to.

TIMOTHY: Look, I'm sorry about the movie.

ANGE: You're a fucking cow ... *[she starts crying.]*

TIMOTHY: I'll buy you a gelato, all right? I'll find a place.

ANGE: Goddamn moo...

TIMOTHY: What did I- ?

ANGE: He's going to die.

TIMOTHY: What?

ANGE: Lame. I dreamed it last night.

TIMOTHY: I thought you didn't...

ANGE: I love him, all right?

TIMOTHY: Lame?

ANGE: Yeah. What? I can love him.

TIMOTHY: Does he know?

ANGE: Are you crazy? He'd fucking kill me.

TIMOTHY: What do you mean?

ANGE: He's a cow. A moo minder.

TIMOTHY: I don't understand...

ANGE: He goes into any hole, drinks up.

TIMOTHY: I see.

ANGE: Do you?

TIMOTHY: But you still love him?

ANGE: I'm crazy as well.

TIMOTHY: ...In this dream...

ANGE: It was horrible. He was all bit up. Like an animal. Flesh in pieces. It's that suit he's seeing: Mesmer. He's no good for him.

He's a bad egg. You know him?

TIMOTHY: No.

ANGE: You made like you did.

TIMOTHY: I don't think so.

ANGE: You made a face.

TIMOTHY: The name, that's all.

ANGE: Some kind of god, isn't it?

TIMOTHY: ...It helps to forget.

ANGE: Convenient amnesia you've got. Mesmer burn your tit, too?

TIMOTHY: There are lives one has. There are lives that exist in ruins, in circular ruins that enclose the heart. They move inside of you, slipping in and out of your memory, in and out of feeling. You watch them. You tuck them away. You excavate them. You see, sometimes you want to bring them back, try them out again. see how that life used to feel inside your skin. But mostly you leave them in ruins.

Cause there's no other place for them anymore. Not in any way you can make sense of.

ANGE: Which life is this?

TIMOTHY: Hmm?

ANGE: Which life are you living now?

TIMOTHY: The one of forgetting.

Lights fade.

Scene twenty

Hospital. Day. ARIADNE sits to one side.

MESMER is awake in bed. LAME is resting on MESMER.

MESMER: I'm fine.

ARIADNE: He's fine.

MESMER: Just my head sometimes...hurts.

ARIADNE: Lame?

MESMER: It'll go away.

ARIADNE: Lame?

MESMER: He's crying.

LAME: I'm not.

MESMER: The boy awakes.

LAME: Don't call me that.

ARIADNE: What else is he going to call you?

LAME: I'm not a boy. I haven't been a boy for years.

MESMER: Don't cry now.

ARIADNE: Such a shame...

LAME: Stop laughing at me.

ARIADNE: He's imagining things.

MESMER: He doesn't look it, but he's got a lively mind. Don't you, Lame?

LAME: Leave off.

MESMER: What did you do with the flowers, eh?

LAME: I tore them up.

ARIADNE: Why did you do that?

LAME: How can you sit there? How can you sit there and look at me?

ARIADNE: I like looking at you. You remind me of things.

LAME: Cock?

ARIADNE: Don't.

MESMER: I'm devoted to Ariadne.

LAME: Yeah? What about me?

MESMER: You tore up my flowers.

LAME: They were no good. They were cheap.

MESMER: I would've liked to have seen them.

LAME: I don't know anything.

ARIADNE: Such a boy...

LAME: You used me.

ARIADNE: We used each other.

LAME: I believed you.

MESMER: The world is full of mystery. Just the other day, I was fine. I was working on my story, meeting deadlines, not thinking of anything.

ARIADNE: Except your dreams.

MESMER: And then my brain snaps, blood runs, oxygen leaves, and I'm here.

ARIADNE: At everyone's mercy.

MESMER: Flowers are left, and I don't even see them. A boy weeps.

LAME: I didn't.

MESMER: I hear things. In my sleep. I even heard Ariadne, even though she didn't show up until...

ARIADNE: I can't stand hospitals.
LAME: I fucking hate them.

MESMER: Nothing can be explained. Not even the fact that I am perfectly fine now.

ARIADNE: You could have another fit.

LAME: Another?

MESMER: There's always the possibility.

LAME: Hell...

MESMER: It's what I live with.

LAME: Will you still see me?

MESMER: I'm seeing you now.

LAME: I mean...

MESMER: Money?

LAME: I don't want anything.

MESMER: Then why don't you leave?

LAME: Everybody around me... they're always screaming, asking for things: girls on the street selling frozen steaks out of plastic bags, knackered boys looking for a bit of a cuddle, old tarts handing me dodgy drinks....I'm nothing. You see? Even Ange. She doesn't believe in me. And I've known her longer than I've known myself.

ARIADNE: What are you saying?

LAME: I feel at peace here.

MESMER: With me?

LAME: You could burn every part of me.

MESMER: What's happened to you, Lame?

LAME: I don't want to lose you.

ARIADNE: You don't know what you're saying.

LAME: Burn me.

ARIADNE: Such a boy...such a shame...

MESMER: Tell me your dreams.

LAME folds into MESMER's arms. Lights fade.

Scene twenty-one

The cramped square of space. NADJA is smoking. TIMOTHY walks in.

NADJA: You've come back?

TIMOTHY: I left my sneaks.

NADJA: I'm smoking. See?

TIMOTHY: There will be nothing left of you.

NADJA: Words don't work anymore. What use are words? They do not educate, they do not change...

TIMOTHY: Where have you put my -?

NADJA: I sat on the train and let him screw me with his inky fingers. I stood on the street and let a car run over a child. I walked into a room and told a boy to undress me so that three men could watch. What are you doing?

TIMOTHY: I'll wear these.

NADJA: Shoes?

TIMOTHY: Why not?

NADJA: They won't fit.

TIMOTHY: They suit me.

NADJA: You'll get lost.

TIMOTHY: I'm already lost.

NADJA: I should have never saved you.

TIMOTHY: You did the right thing.

NADJA: So you could leave?

TIMOTHY: I go to the movies, Nadja. Every day. I see slasher movies. First show is at eleven in the morning, last one at midnight. I watch them all. At the multi-plex, at the corner cinema where the vinyl seats stick to your ass, wherever I can...Slasher movies are my favorite. I've seen three hundred deaths this week. And next week, I'll see more. I can't stop.

NADJA: You're killing yourself.

TIMOTHY: I've stopped smoking.

NADJA: Have you?

TIMOTHY: Nothing but amyl nitrate and ice cream now.

NADJA: Together?

TIMOTHY: Sometimes it's the only way I can come.

NADJA: You're crazy.

TIMOTHY: I feel alive, Nadja.

NADJA: Lace your shoes. You'll fall like that.

TIMOTHY: They are laced.

NADJA: Missed a hole.

TIMOTHY: Where?

NADJA: You eyes don't work right yet.

TIMOTHY: I'll be all right.

NADJA: You'll fall all over yourself.

TIMOTHY: I'll use some of this tape, fix the laces in place.

NADJA: You shouldn't be out walking.

TIMOTHY: I saw a movie the other day. I looked at the screen and saw myself.

NADJA: What'd you mean?

TIMOTHY: It wasn't advertised, this movie... It didn't have a name. The reel must've slipped in somehow. There was the sound of a crash, wheels screeching, the screen went black for a second, then it's me.

NADJA: You?

TIMOTHY: Up on the screen. Like a fucking star. Walking out of a car on a bare road with blood all over my trousers. I think it's Berlin because I hear a voice. Someone is speaking in German. The voice belongs to a woman.

The woman is laughing. I turn around. The screen goes black again. There is the sound of a car door opening. Light fills the screen. Radiant colors. I am standing by the guard-rail on the road. I'm looking down. There's the sound of speeding cars and the voice of the woman.

I can't see my eyes. It is as if they have been eaten by the sun. The blood on my trousers is dry. The woman's voice calls to me "Timothy?" There are legs and hands below me. There are fingers missing. I look closer, keeping my foot on the rail. They are the legs of boys, age twelve, thirteen...dead boys...

The woman calls to me again "Timothy?" I turn to her. I cannot see her face. The camera moves. My foot slams against the rail. I feel as if I am falling. The screen goes black, and when light returns, only the car can be seen. Neither the woman nor the man, which is me, can be found. Are you listening to me?

NADJA: You saw a movie.

TIMOTHY: The man on the screen was me. It was your voice, Nadja.

NADJA: I don't speak German.

TIMOTHY: Who did we crash into?

NADJA: We didn't crash into anything.

TIMOTHY: Why do you lie to me?

NADJA: I mis-use affection. But I don't lie.

TIMOTHY: From the day you met me.

Aiming that camera at me, calling to me, sinking your tongue into my mouth,

messing up my hair.

NADJA: I didn't mean anything. I just wanted to-

TIMOTHY: Locking me up in this room, bringing me cold food to eat. Stealing all my things: my sneakers, my back-pack. What did you think you were going to do with me?

NADJA: I wanted to protect you. I wanted to... hold you.

TIMOTHY: Fucking... make me sick.

Give me your mouth.

NADJA: ?

TIMOTHY: No more lies.

TIMOTHY tapes NADJA's mouth shut. Dark.

Scene twenty-two

The cramped square of space, which feels narrower now. Half-light. MESMER cradles NADJA. Her wrists and ankles have also been bound with tape. She remains gagged, from previous.

MESMER: Are you crying? Is that what you do when your lover leaves? Dry your eyes. Stop now. The tape is wet. You'll ruin everything.

Come. Let's set you down over here. The light will not come into your eyes.

He sets her down in another part of the room.

It's safer here. Away from the window.

You don't know what could come through that window. Does your body hurt, dear? Are your joints tired of being locked? You shouldn't cry. It only makes things worse. You know that better than anyone. Don't you, Nadja? I've seen you. You stood by the road as the boys went down. You recorded everything. What makes anyone keep their eyes fixed on atrocity? Do you take pleasure in it? I take pleasure everyday. In bits. You see this boy?

Light reveals LAME in a corner.

There are cigarette burns all over his naked body.

He came to me. One day. Unknowing. A transaction. That's all he was. A little hell-child off the street. He let me touch him. He let me do my will. Look at him. He can't even look at me without drowning his eyes...I can't touch him anymore. There is no part of him that is unknown to me. I found every bit of pleasure I could. Stop shaking, Lame. Stop looking at me.

I give him to you, Nadja. I offer him to you. Do with him what you will. He' my sacrifice.

I'll take the camera now, and the slice of film where the minotaur's face can be seen.

You've been good to keep it here. To keep it for me. It will help me write my story, the story of seven boys killed...Thank you for everything.

MESMER picks up camera and exits.

LAME slowly makes his way toward NADJA. Lights fade.

Scene twenty-three

The square space. Time has passed.

Light falls from the window and onto NADJA and LAME's bodies. NADJA is unbound. LAME rests, near her. He remains naked. Silence.

NADJA: Bubble.

LAME: Bubble.

NADJA: Do you like it?

LAME: It's a good word.

NADJA: Try another.

LAME: Don't know...

NADJA: Try another.

LAME: Can't think...

Pause.

NADJA: Plenty.

LAME: Plenty?

NADJA: Yes.

LAME: I don't like it.

NADJA: Try another.

LAME: Sorrow.

NADJA: Sorrow?

LAME: Yes.

NADJA: There's no room for it.

LAME: Leave it on your tongue.

NADJA: Sorrow.

Pause.

LAME: It's a word my Mom used. I remember.

NADJA: I can't remember my mother.

LAME: She made custard pies, and creamy strawberries.

NADJA: I can't remember anything before Timothy.

LAME: Who's that?

NADJA: Someone I knew.

LAME: I'm hungry.

NADJA: Sorrow...

Pause.

LAME: Kiss me.

NADJA: Can't.

LAME: Lips hurt?

NADJA: Everything does.

LAME: Same as me.

NADJA: I'm not...

LAME: The same.

NADJA: You fall in love. Not me.

LAME: What about Timothy?

NADJA: I try not to think.

LAME: Loved him, didn't you?

NADJA: Out in the open.

LAME: He left you here, in this squat.

NADJA: So did Mesmer.

LAME: I wanted him to.

NADJA: You could barely breathe.

LAME: I asked him to destroy me.

NADJA: Sick with love.

LAME: I didn't want to feel anything anymore.

NADJA: Through with feeling?

LAME: Yes.

NADJA: Everyone lies.

Pause.

LAME: I wonder where Ange... *(Slight moment)* Give me a word.

NADJA: Empty.

LAME: Empty.

Lights fade.

Scene twenty-four

NADJA watches LAME sleep. She sings to him "In the Stolen Part.".

NADJA: Would you give a toss

If all was lost?

Would you still look out for me?

In the stolen part of my...

LAME stirs. He is crying. She stops singing.

Shh.

She continues singing.

You could be...

Dark.

Scene twenty-five

High-rise. Wide view of the city.

MESMER is writing. ARIADNE stands, looking out onto the expanse of city below.

ARIADNE: I'll miss Lame.

MESMER: You were jealous of him.

ARIADNE: At first. Yes. I wanted to kill you. But after the hospital... There was nothing to say, was there? He was just a boy. I could see that. He only wanted a bit of pain, a bit of meaning in his life.

MESMER: Like the boys on the news.

ARIADNE: They found him, you know.

MESMER: Who?

ARIADNE: The killer, the butcher...The Minotaur. A man out of uniform shot him through the eye, punctured his spine. The beast fell.

MESMER: No more dreams...

ARIADNE: You've posted your story?

MESMER: Everything's sorted now.

ARIADNE: ...I would've liked to have seen him.

MESMER: The Minotaur?

ARIADNE: His face.

MESMER: What for?

ARIADNE: So I could put him in my dreams. Along with the boys. I like everything to have its place. You taught me that.

MESMER: Have I?

ARIADNE: And Lame.

MESMER: Still jealous.

ARIADNE: I'd like someone to hide me in their wing.

Pause.

MESMER: Sky's turning.

ARIADNE: Looks like Barcelona.

MESMER: We should go. How long has it been...?

ARIADNE: Honeymoon.

MESMER: Did we...?

ARIADNE: Don't you remember?

MESMER: The Twin Hotels.

ARIADNE: On the sand.

MESMER: We baked.

ARIADNE: Fried our skin.

MESMER: We offered ourselves up.

ARIADNE: To the gods?

MESMER: To everything.

Lights fade as the city gleams.

Scene twenty-six

A side street. TIMOTHY and ANGE are bruised.

TIMOTHY: Sucked my fingers. Licked your crack.

ANGE: Paid up, didn't he?

TIMOTHY: If he hadn't cuffed me, I would've beat him. I'm getting old. Too old for this.

ANGE: What'd you mean?

TIMOTHY: What am I doing with you?

ANGE: We have a laugh.

TIMOTHY: I want something more.

ANGE: Go back to Nadja.

TIMOTHY: You don't know her.

ANGE: Is she a good egg?

TIMOTHY: Found me on the street, gave me sweets. Gave me words. "Bubble." A round word. It filled me up. She said "Slow doon." We'd fuck all night, and she'd just hold onto me. We were on the road, my foot was on the guardrail, there was a man coming up to me.

It was as if he knew every part of me. But I couldn't place where I had met him

ANGE: Another life?

TIMOTHY: Nadja pulled at me, tugged at my Teletubbie, tucked me under her arm.

We flew over a million cities – Berlin, Glasgow, New York...I could see everything – intersections and tollbooths and boys pissing on the street; There was blood on my trousers, and glass in my eyes. "Hold on," Nadja said. "Hang on, love." And we kept flying over nameless cities, as the man's face turned away from me. Nadja set me down in a room. I wanted to hold her all the time. Even if I didn't know where I was. What does it matter where one is anyway if you have to spend all your time watching people die?

ANGE: ...I'll buy you a frock. From the boutique. Vintage Alexander McQueen.

TIMOTHY: I don't want one.

ANGE: How about a helmet?

TIMOTHY: Why would I want that?

ANGE: They're expensive.

Pause.

TIMOTHY: They found the man. The one who killed the boys.

ANGE: You knew him?

TIMOTHY: Why do you say that?

ANGE: Sounded like you did, the way you said it.

TIMOTHY: He was a stranger. Let out from some institution. They say he had a knot under his tongue.

ANGE: You believe that?

TIMOTHY: It was online.

ANGE: Rubbish.

TIMOTHY: It will be safe now.

ANGE: You're dreaming.

TIMOTHY: Safe from him.

ANGE: ...What am I going to do with all this money?

TIMOTHY: Get an ice cream.

Lights fade as TIMOTHY walks away.

Scene twenty-seven

The cramped square of space. Graffiti on the walls has faded.

LAME and NADJA face out. He is wearing Nadja's blouse. She is wearing one of Timothy's shirts, and a skirt.

NADJA: I filmed children. I watched them through the lens. Different schools, different cities.

LAME: Why'd you stop?

NADJA: Went in one day, all the children in the school had been shot.

LAME: You film it?

NADJA: I started to turn my camera on everything after that. I struck a bargain with God. I looked Him in the eye and said "I will conquer death by looking at it over and over again." I went from one city to the other until I found this room, where I thought I would not have to conquer anything.

LAME: Quiet.

NADJA: I don't know now what it is I see.

If I stop the images in my brain, what's left me?

LAME: There's a game I used to play.

NADJA: No games. Please.

LAME: Hand over eyes. Go on. Don't be afraid.

NADJA: I can't...

LAME: I'll do it with you. *[He places his hand over his eyes]* One, two...

NADJA: Where'd you learn this game?

LAME: When I was a boy and all the pretty-ugly lads would take turns screwing me.

Go on. Count.

NADJA: One...two...

LAME: Keep your hands over your eyes. Take your time.

NADJA continues counting silently, then....

NADJA: I think I could walk out of this room with my bones aching, and I wouldn't care what would find me.

LAME: I'm not afraid. I'm not afraid of anything.

NADJA: It's like when I was ten years old.

LAME: On the beach. No sand. Just pebbles. Wind beats. And the change machine at the arcade spits out Euros by the hundreds, and everyone is playing. Bowie blasting through the speakers with his mad-idle face looking at me, bare and gleaming. And I want him in my mouth, between my legs. I want the Euros in my hand to buy me everything.

NADJA: Ten years old and I can't even see the beach. There is only land here. Tall hills. And leaves I collect with my bare hands. I try to pretend I am somewhere else. Sometimes I forget the words to things. The leaves are full of dirt. I carry them with me.

LAME: I got mirrors on my nipples, and black galaxy varnish on my toes. Everything glitters: my eyes, hair, tits... It's time to nick a little, steal a little... light.

NADJA: [counting] Fifteen...

LAME: I see a poster for Barcelona on the walkway. I can't feel the holes that have been burned into me. I am unmarked, un-broken.

NADJA: I see a poster for Barcelona on the walkway, outside the door, on the other side of the street. This is somewhere I have never been.

LAME: Barcelona.

NADJA: Barcelona.

LAME: A mobile rings in the distance.

NADJA: Don't answer anything. The world doesn't need any more stories of slain children

LAME: and slain beasts. I walk slowly.

NADJA: Out of the labyrinth...

The room falls away, no walls, no windows.

Warm Catalan sun beats down. MESMER appears.

MESMER: I dreamed I was in a city that was a dream.

NADJA: What did you see?

MESMER: I saw you looking at me when I was dead to feeling. You came to me holding a camera to my heart, and said

NADJA: Enter me in your dream.

MESMER: And the atlas turned, and the skies shivered, and we remembered pieces of ourselves

NADJA: Bits we had left behind

MESMER: Lives we had abandoned because we wanted to destroy everything.

Pause.

NADJA: Out of this,

MESMER: out of this,

NADJA: out of this world...

MESMER: Everything is within our compass.

NADJA: *[Simultaneous]*... Let's make...

MESMER: *[Simultaneous]*... Let's make...

A senseless act

NADJA: of beauty...

MESMER and NADJA begin to devour LAME.

Light bathes them, then fades.

End of Play

THE TROPIC OF X

(after *Orpheus* and *Euridice*)

by

CARIDAD SVICH

Script History:

This script was principally developed with support of the TCG/Pew National Theatre Artist Residency program, with additional support from the Radcliffe Institute for Advanced Study at Harvard University. It received a mini-workshop at INTAR in New York City in the fall of 2003 under Michael John Garces' direction, and a reading at Rattlestick Playwrights Theater in New York City under Debbie Saivetz's direction as part of their Exposure Festival. It also received development time and space at the University of Iowa Department of Theatre Arts, and Arizona State University-Tempe Department of Theatre Arts. A revised version of the play was presented by the 2005 Latino Play Reading Series at [Inside] the Ford, CA under Stefan Novinski's direction, and at Teatro Vista-Chicago in their Tapas Reading Series under Derrick Sander's direction. The play was first runner-up in the 2005 Pen is a Mighty Sword Competition sponsored by Virtual Theater Project and Wake Forest University. It will receive its English-language premiere with Single Carrot Theatre in Baltimore, Maryland in 2013.

The play received its professional premiere in a German-language translation by Stefanie Fiedler and Molly Shaiken at ARTheater-Cologne, Germany as a co-production between lowskin productions (Cologne) and Immigrants Theatre Project (New York City) which opened on May 31st, 2007. It was directed by Marcy Arlin; the music/sound design was by Kai Niggemann; video installation by Klaus Dietermann; lighting design by Johannes Kordes; other members of the scenic and costume and tech/production design: Tina Toeberg, Irakli Kiziria, Carmela Mascia, Christiane Molan, Jurgen Pistol; dramaturg was Renee Knapp; the line producers for ARTheater were Andreas Robertz and Bernd Rehse. The cast was as follows:

Hilton . . . . . . Ben Steinhoff

Mori . . . . . . Stephen Appleton

Maura . . . . . . Heidrun Reinhardt

Kiki . . . . . . Sunga Weineck

Fabian/Frankie . . . . . . Bernd Rehse

Video trailers of the ARTheater-Cologne production can be found at

http://www.youtube.com/watch?v=nGEDybsCwig

and http://www.youtube.com/watch?v=TcZX1JtSLHQ

Characters:

HILTON, DJ cowboy of the island airwaves

MAURA, arcade junkie and petite wannabe assassin in faux Docs,

MORI, Maura's accomplice and lover

KIKI, part-time hustler of fluid gender (preferably played by a man);

FABIAN, a tourist in many guises; also plays FRANKIE, a man who watches the road

The Setting:

In the polyglot Americas, leaning south: a market of video arcades, old and new drugs, Nescafe internet cafes, swift-changing political regimes, fluctuating currency, cheap sex for the tourist trade, ex-bullrings turned into discos and hotels, white cars and bright blue houses with peeling paint, fresh murals on ruined walls, and a view of the limitless, dirty sea.

Notes:

Occasional Spanish words and phrases are italicized in the script, as are other non-English-language phrases. Melodies to the original songs featured in the text may be obtained by contacting the author, or lyrics may be re-set by another composer.

Part One

1: Hilton, the Cowboy of the islands, Broadcasts to the world

HILTON: *Oye oye oye oye oye oye oye*

This is the voice

The voice

The voice...

This is the voice of radio *Dos Equis*

in the A, B, D and number four,

you hear me?

This is the electric boogaloo

of the cowboy of the islands

who seeks remedy,

remedy and fast,

for his ailing everything

because everything is broken down

down

and way down

in the triple crown

of the Mayor and Governor

and all the Powerful with the capital P.

The microphone is defunct, you see?

And everything has gone K-side,

As in by the wayside

waylaid

and outside the official news.

The Z doesn't work. For nothing.

You hear me?

The Z is absent, failing, stretched out limbless and waiting for X

as in *Dos Equis*

as in as much as you can take.

In which language

do you want me to speak?

There is no one language

or haven't you heard *del* Babel

in which we live?

This is the new Babylonia and it is grand.

So grand you can't even remember what you said after you've said it.

We're in an inferno like Dante's. Remember him? Dante knew everything. He was prescient.

He was one of those super-intellectuals

who ate it and good.

Because he told it how it was, is and will be,

and we're just following.

You hear me?

In this language mangled and spit

I speak to you

Like two and two are six!

And no one can stop me

cause I still got my tongue.

No one can stop me

cause I still got my tongue.

No one can stop me

cause I still got my tongue.

2: The arcade junkies, Maura and Mori, look at the tourist

MAURA: Look at him.

MORI: Quit.

MAURA: Juicy fruit

MORI: Enough.

MAURA: Hey, juicy fruit, I'm going to eat you.

MORI: Leave him alone.

MAURA: Why?

MORI: He's a tourist.

MAURA: Tourist in the land of plastic elastic mescaline rush.

MORI: You'll scare him.

MAURA: He's already scared. We should assault him now and get it over with.

MORI: What for?

MAURA: To confirm his suspicions about traveling where he doesn't belong.

MORI: How do you know he doesn't belong?

MAURA: He's wearing a hat.

MORI: I wear a hat.

MAURA: Not like that. He's wearing – what? – some retro thingy. He thinks he's in some foreign movie, some tropical exotica fascist propaganda flick. Who are you playing, juicy fruit?

MORI: Leave him be.

MAURA: Why should I?

MORI: It's early.

MAURA: And what? You got something better to do, Mori?

MORI: I'm kicking back.

MAURA: Like a little yogurt cup. Like a little mango-guava delight. Soft belly. Soft arms. You're weak.

MORI: I work out.

MAURA: In what gym?

MORI: The gymnasium of the mind.

MAURA: Mental hoops and loop-de-loops?

MORI: Too advanced for you, Maura?

MAURA: Hey, I'm not a fashionista *turista*. I studied, right? Hey, *turista*, give me a juicy fruit. Damn holding onto his gum. Northern pig.

MORI: He's not from the North. He's Euro.

MAURA: Euro Deustche?

MORI: Euro something. Check his shoes.

MAURA: They're good shoes.

MORI: Not Docs [Doc Martens], but good. Pure cow.

MAURA: His feet must be hot in them.

MORI: No. With good shoes your feet never get hot.

MAURA: Perfect temperature, eh?

MORI: Year-round.

MAURA: We should steal them.

MORI: The shoes?

MAURA: Yeah.

MORI: Why?

MAURA: Screw him up. Destabilize him.

MORI: Kick him better.

MAURA: Yeah, kick him too. But take the shoes.

MORI: How are you going to do that?

MAURA: How do we do anything?

MORI: With *cojones*.

MAURA: *Cojones*. Yeah.

MORI: Smarts.

MAURA: Mental agility dexterity. That's right. Tricks and scams.

MORI: You know them all, Maura.

MAURA: So do you, Mori. Don't act like you're so innocent.

MORI: I like being innocent.

MAURA: Scratch your face off the map of youth, my friend.

MORI: Hurt me.

MAURA: I wound you. Soft Mori, my little yogurt cup. Give me some.

MORI: What are you talking - ?

MAURA: Tongue, animal.

MORI: My tongue is mine. I do with it what I will.

MAURA: Who are you holding out for?

MORI: ...Princess Di.

MAURA: You're getting all vampire necrophiliac.

MORI: I'm not.

MAURA: Then who? Who is it you're dreaming of in your star-gazy moon?

MORI: Christina...whatsit.

MAURA: Britney effsit?

MORI: I like blondes, all right?

MAURA: I can be platinum.

MORI: I mean natural blondes. They taste music.

MAURA: They're not in your league, *pelon*.

MORI: Don't call me that.

MAURA: You don't like me anymore? You don't like Maura with the firm tits? What happened, eh? You're swinging the other way now?

MORI: ...I smell, okay?

MAURA: Since when did that stop you? Hey, Euro, what's your name? Why don't you look at me, huh? You don't like chicks like me? *Matador*.

MORI: What are you saying?

MAURA: He's a *pato patinski*.

MORI: Don't look it.

MAURA: Screwy Euro. We should jump him now. We should annihilate him like an effing Ninja matrix warrior. Screw this hanging around looking at the ocean doing nothing waiting to drown crap.

MORI: You're crazy.

MAURA: Crazy carioca cherry Coke-a.

MORI: What goes on inside your head, Maura?

MAURA: Tunnel. Like when you race through all dark and stuff and you can't see anything but you see everything, right? Like a digital robotic fast forward whoosh in the mini-wave of a microwave.

MORI: Like the dreams of an emperor of a third world catastrophe?

MAURA: You get me.

MORI: I read you.

MAURA: You're inside my mind, Mori. Lick me. Peel my grape.

MORI: I'm kicking...

MAURA: You're a street *pendejo* with mental *congri* in your brain and no Euros.

MORI: Who wants Euros?

MAURA: I do. I want a tasty Euro in my pocket to give me an effing big screen adventure that will last me the next one hundred years of goddamned solitude in the global solitude of my aching capitalist soul. You hear me, juicy?

MORI: Why do I hang with you, Maura?

MAURA: Cause you like me, Mori. We're good for each other.

MORI: Are we?

MAURA: ...Let's kick his ass. Come on. I'm sick of staying here. I'm sick of looking at this endless ocean, this water of death waiting for nothing. Let him know what being a tourist is really like. Let's give him what he came for.

And Maura and Mori go after the tourist with restless vengeance screaming in their lungs.

They want to feel their strength, and release themselves from the hard drive in which they are packed.

Pierce,

break,

split open

the man in the strange hat who wears his pride as casually as his fine leather shoes.

3: From another view Kiki looks on in dreams

KIKI: I want to die here. Right here.

There's no-where else to die.

You hear me?

[if] You want another place

you got to keep your head straight

and your back against the wall.

This is the fifth of all avenues.

I can see everything here.

I have the perfect view.

You wear a hat that sticks out.

You look at me and dream.

And I dream with you.

This is me altogether in the flesh.

Come on. Rub me. Harder.

Oh, honey, you don't know what you're doing.

You got it all wrong about me.

I'm special, ok? I'm one of those...

they don't got a name for me cause I'm too special,

that's how special I am,

you know what I'm saying?

Here in flames I speak to you.

Here in flesh I come to you.

Call me, baby. Call me.

I'm your friend. Like the arcade angels say...

they're on the other side of the street.

They protect me.

They have wings. Steel wings.

There are no secrets here, baby.

And when you mistreat me, cause you will,

cause that's what you do, that's what they all do,

I won't say anything.

No, honey. I'll just... I'll be friendly.

Okay? Okay? Okay?

I will die here.

Right here.

Because there's nothing else to live for.

nothing else to dress for.

Nothing...

4: Mori and Maura exalt

MORI: He was

MAURA: Like he didn't even...

MORI: Blink twitch nothing.

MAURA: Coward.

MORI: Queasy bastard.

MAURA: Did you see how he - ?

MORI: Yeah. He thought you were –

MAURA: A poor waif-*ona*.

MORI: You showed him.

MAURA: Dig in, Euro man. With teeth.

MORI: And legs.

MAURA: And boots. I got rev boots.

MORI: Fake Docs.

MAURA: Faux Docs. The best kind. Straight from Rio by way of London. Why get an original anything when everything's a spin-off?

MORI: We should hit the arcade.

MAURA: Jet-ski in virtual land. Hitting the hills, cyber-snow skidding, testing our balance like guerrilla punk skazis.

MORI: And go from one machine to the other, one screen to the other like raging cowboys of the new wave.

MAURA: The next wave. Cowboys with no land to call their own. Cowboys of the vanguard.

MORI: Living in a desert of laptops and concrete churches called malls. Oh Virgin, oh Sony, oh Swatch most holy.

MAURA: I can't go to the mall. Not now.

MORI: Why not?

MAURA: I'm too wired. That uptight upright tourist with the funny hat burned me up. Nothing but looking me over, up and down. He thought "I can do with her what I like."

MORI: You showed him.

MAURA: That's right. Maura is not noise. Maura is real sound.

Kiki cuts in.

KIKI: What about me, eh?

MAURA: Get away, Kiki.

KIKI: I'm just looking for scraps, Maura.

MAURA: You're such a sorry-ass girly girl.

KIKI: I'm hundred percent male, honey. No eggs in my basket.

MAURA: You got eyes like piss holes in the snow, though.

KIKI: My eyes have character. Unlike yours. You could use some shadow, honey. You're so plain.

MAURA: It suits me.

KIKI: You won't get a man that way.

MAURA: I don't need a man. I have Mori.

MORI: Is that a cut? Are you cutting me?

KIKI: She's complimenting you, honey. Can't you tell a compliment when you hear one?

MORI: I don't like compliments. I don't trust them. If somebody compliments you, look out, cause what they want is something in return.

KIKI: And what's wrong with that?

MORI: Debt. I don't like to be in someone's debt.

MAURA: I'm not asking for anything, Mori.

MORI: Good. Cause you won't get.

MAURA: I'm the love of your life, remember? Or don't you remember?... Once upon a time...There lived what?

MORI: ...Maura.

MAURA: And Mori. Mori and Maura. Joined at the hip lip no matter what sinking ship, right?

MORI: ...Right.

MAURA: Screw you.

MORI: What?

MAURA: I'm all in a rush, and look what you do. You bring me down, Mori. Completely down like in a well and I'm going to drown.

KIKI: Stop with that drowning crap. It doesn't suit you, honey. You're not cut out for pity.

MAURA: And you are?

KIKI: I've got the thighs, baby.

MORI: I like your thighs, Kiki. They're strong.

KIKI: Scissor-legs, honey. That's me. I wrap you in my scissor legs and the world rests a little better.

MAURA: Would you stop...

KIKI: I'm not doing anything.

MAURA: I got Mori, right? Mori and me, we're a team. You got whomever. Okay?

KIKI: What's with the rules, honey?

MORI: Maura likes rules.

MAURA: I'm feeling good, right? You know how long it takes for me to feel good? So, don't mess, all right? Don't get in my stuff.

KIKI: You're getting very sensitive, Maura.

MAURA: And I've saved your ass I don't how many times, Kiki. Even's even. Fair's fair. (*Pause.*)

I can't look at the sky anymore.

KIKI: You don't have to look at it, baby.

MAURA: Liquid painted blue. Crystal blue. Perfect blue. Too damn perfect.

KIKI: Maura, you drown in a glass of water.

MAURA: I do what I like.

KIKI: I do what I like, too.

MAURA: Begging for looks. Morning, noon and night Kiki has to be ready for any cold suit who speaks the *lingua franca*.

MORI: Or the *franca lengua*.

MAURA: Tongue yeah. Sweaty stinky from yesterday's milk.

MORI: The honest tongue, the frank tongue who gets in...

MAURA: And doesn't stop.

MORI: Working it, working it, working it.

MAURA: And then "Oh, Kiki, oh, Kiki, what is that between your legs, baby?

MORI: "Oh, let me stick my tongue in anyway cause we're like Tristan and Isolde, baby. When we make love, we lose ourselves and become each other."

KIKI: I didn't know you were an opera diva, Mori.

MORI: I'm not.

KIKI: Then why Tristan, honey? Why Isolde?

MORI: It was a web link on a site I was surfing.

KIKI: Maura and Mori: the two freaks.

MAURA: Well, at least I'm not standing around all "hey, want to see me, check me out, Check this, hey."

KIKI: You're high society, eh?

MORI: She's from aristocracy.

MAURA: Quit.

MORI: Her great-grandfather was the Prince of Old *Vayazul*.

MAURA: Shut up, Mori.

MORI: What? *Vayazul* doesn't even exist anymore. It's 19th century. We shot down those memories a long time ago.

KIKI: Who needs memories when you got TV?

MORI: Exactly. The stories we need we got. They're given to us. Replay ad infinitum.

KIKI: Even those of the Prince of Old *Vayazul*.

MAURA: Look, I don't want to be disappeared, allright? Look, I don't want to be disappeared, all right? I don't want to be put in prison. I don't want to have to smuggle myself inside a merchandise van or boat to get the hell out. When the last coup happened, I burned any reference to my great-grandfather that I had. I'm here. I do what I do. I choose my life. I make it.

KIKI: How serious.

MAURA: What's wrong with being serious, eh? Everything has to be a party? Everything has to be a cool easy flip surface trip? I'm tired of it. I get tired. I'm not a twenty-four-seven wind-up doll watch her go. You want to amuse yourselves, go to the arcade, go to the peep show, go to the strip n' screw on the boardwalk, leave me alone.

KIKI: Maura, you worry me.

MAURA: Why's that, Kiki?

KIKI: It's like you want to run for office or something.

MAURA: Like running for office means something. The country's been fixed from day one. Prop one puppet up, take him down, prop up another. Everything's the same.

KIKI: Rules change.

MAURA: One day you're on the left, the next on the right. And so the story spins...

MORI: You just have to make sure you know which side you're on.

MAURA: Before they change sides, yeah. And when you're at bottom, you better know everything. Cause bottom-feeders are the first to get screwed, cause we're disposable.

KIKI: We're not.

MAURA: Trash-stuffers. Not even trash. But trash-stuffers, that's what we are.

MORI: Speak for yourself.

MAURA: You're above things, Mori?

MORI: Hell yeah. I'm not disposable. I got words, right? I can say things, do things.

MAURA: We're the X corner of the alphabet.

KIKI: Says the great-princess of Old *Vayazul*.

MAURA: Take Maura down for being who she is. Is that what you want? I could wrap you right now. Cord round your neck and you'd be out. No more crap words from you.

...

You're not even worth killing. You're not worth pop bang ouch. Flame girl. Flame nobody, that's what you are: a cog in the wheel of the economic meltdown of the effing meltdowns of this bronco busting rodeo barrio society.

KIKI: ...I wish I came from something. My family is not even a headline. Not a mention would they get. They're from a little village on the coast. Barely a village. One of those K-side towns nobody cares about. Cars come through and they keep going, you know, they don't stop. I'm Kiki. I'm a little flea in this city. Who cares about Kiki?

MORI: I do.

KIKI: Mori, you're always there with a compliment.

MAURA: Only when he doesn't mean it.

KIKI: You have some bug up your *yo-no-se-que*?

MAURA: No bug.

KIKI: You know what you are? You're a phobic.

You act all free and all that but deep down you're old school. Someone is a little different and you get all shook up, out of orbit.

MAURA: I do not.

KIKI: Then why the 'tude, baby? Why against me?

MAURA: I like messing with you.

MORI: It's a sign of affection. She does it with me all the time.

KIKI: Plant me a wet one, then. I need confirmation, baby. I need to know who I'm with. I'm not interested in hanging around with phobics, you know. I got enough of that to last me plenty.

MAURA: You want a kiss, I'll give it. What's a kiss among friends?

KIKI: A sweet kiss.

Maura and Kiki kiss.

MORI: [*a fragment of an old poem recalled*]

Sweet at waking, sing the young from the cradle.

Sweet at waking, ancient solitude.

Kiss ends.

MAURA: How poetic-o.

MORI: I'm more than crap.

MAURA: And who said you weren't?

MORI: I don't know sometimes.

KIKI: Where are you from, Mori?

MORI: What do you mean?

KIKI: You're from somewhere, right? A town, village?

MORI: Yeah. So?

KIKI: Well, then, where from?

MORI: Why do you ask? Do I have an accent or something?

KIKI: It's just a question..

MORI: I don't like questions like that. They're stupid. They make no sense. I don't have an accent. I don't even have a twang. Why do you ask me that?

KIKI: I didn't know you were so sensitive. Between you and Maura, I don't know where to stand. (*Pause. Kiki observes at the stolen shoes.*)

MAURA: Get your eyes off my things, Kiki.

KIKI: Oh, are these yours?

MORI: They were the tourist's.

KIKI: Is that all you got from him?

MAURA: That was the goal.

KIKI: Well, what are you going to do with them?

MORI: We could go to the country, sell them to a farm family. They always need shoes.

KIKI: The man had a watch, no? He had money.

MORI: He had a hat.

KIKI: If you're going to assault someone, do it right.

MAURA: I did. I kicked his face in. I took his corporate ass down, eh?

KIKI: And what did you do, Mori? What contribution did you make to this phenomenal escapade?

MORI: I spit on him.

KIKI: Well, that's very... ancient law.

MORI: You're dragging my ass, Kiki.

MAURA: That's all she ever does.

KIKI: Hey, don't be so hard on me, honeys. You like Kiki to be around. (*Kiki reveals cocaine bag.*)

While you two were spitting at your tourist, I pocketed a little something from my coffee man.

MORI: The Venetian guy.

KIKI: Milan, baby.

MORI: Oh, right, the Milan guy who's staying at the Roc.

MAURA: [is it] Fresh?

KIKI: Give me a little credit, honey.

MAURA: How much do you want?

KIKI: What'd you mean?

MAURA: You ain't showing fresh powder for nothing.

KIKI: I'm egalitarian. I like sharing with my friends....If you don't want it, you don't want it.

MORI: Give.

KIKI: Hungry Mori. Bite, Mori. Bite me. You're my vampire, baby. You're my loco loco-motion.

MORI: Give me everything.

5: In the rush the cowboy of the islands is on air

HILTON: And here in the Z

We rush and rush to forget who we are

Because who cares who we are

We are ephemera ephemeral

Birds passing

Birds in flight

Birds singing songs *por un Diablo*

For a poor *triste* devil who will rescue us.

Rescue me, please, from this eternal oblivion

From this *mala noche*

That has upset my dreams.

"Rescue me," like the old song says,

and don't make me pay for it.

Cause we have enough dues.

We have dues to last a hundred centuries.

How long must we pay? How long?

For tobacco, sugar, rice, bamboo,

tango, mambo y *agua azul?*

[testifying] It has been too long

and my back is breaking from the weight

And the expectation of your caress so free.

Sound my ecstasy, love incomplete.

The cymbals are loud.

The flood comes,

and we take one look at ourselves

and drown.

The cowboy of the islands, twirls an invisible lasso, and practices his rodeo tricks to a song from a long-ago Western isle.

6: Kiki is witness to Mori and Maura getting amped up; in counterpoint she offers the not-so-secret history of powder (a pop-up)

KIKI: Baby loose fine

Basuco cane

Gutter glitter

Bubble bunk

Coca is not cocaine.

She has been given a bad name.

Zip

Witch

Coconut

Jelly

Merk

Rock

Pimp

Stardust belly

Coca is placed on the mouth.

The leaf is chewed.

The pinch of lime soothes

In Bolivia, Columbia, Venezuela and Peru.

Have a dust

Hitch up the reindeer

Send your Inca message to Jim Jones,

Aunt Nora

Homer

Bernice

Roxanne

And the Chippy chola

The cotton brothers

Get lost, and amped

In the Florida snow

And geeze the junk in the last screw,

In this last screw for Johnny

Midst the Diablito dust.

Coca is a tonic. Coca tempers.

We all love our Coca-Cola.

Give me sweet Coca-Cola. We hum and hum.

But then in 1903

cocaine was taken out of Coca-Cola,

And our hum got low, down

and the joy was kicked out

until 1914

when cocaine became illegal in the United States.

No more coca, the governor said, the mayor said, the policeman said, the general said.

The ban was placed.

And so a new currency was born,

that helped boost the economies

of Bolivia, Peru, Columbia and Venezuela.

Good for us. Good and plenty.

We will keep you coming and going for eternity.

And cocaine was smuggled in shoes

In condoms

In empty bellies

and brandy,

in baby powder so fine so loose so dandy.

Such fine powder

we could never hope to find anywhere else.

And networks were set up country to country

The geography expanded upon demand

And we saluted the monopoly,

The nouveau artistocracy,

The potent democracy of trade on trade.

The buy and sell,

And the juiced up high octane chain

From Columbia through Poland to Italy,

from the UK to Holland to Kansas City,

from Moscow to Peru to Argentina,

from Oklahoma to Miami to new Arcadia.

Oh, Spain, oh Portugal, coca breathes.

Hosanna of the most heavenly currency.

Protect me, oh Morpheus, god of dreams.

7: Maura tracks the tourists with her telescope eyes while Mori sleeps off the powder

MAURA: The one with the scarf.

The one with the tie.

Which one? Which one shall I take?

MORI: Huh?

MAURA: The one with the bracelet.

The one with the attaché case.

Which one? Which one shall I take?

MORI: What?

MAURA: The one with the ring.

The one with the diamond bar tie-clip

and the bottle of spring?

MORI: You know...Go....

MAURA: Wait for me, Mori. Wait.

Maura goes in search of another tourist.

8: And Kiki picks up the shoes

KIKI: Sweet Mori, how sweet you are.

Sleeping without incident, without a care dare.

Did you hear the shoot-out, honey?

Did you hear the screams?

There were guns, Mori. Out on the street.

They killed somebody. I heard them.

Honey, everything is K-side, don't you know?

And we go on, like nothing's changed,

sleeping like restless tigers,

acting like everything's going to be fine..

When I move my mouth, I think of Antarctica.

I see myself in a cold climate with snow

and a frozen lake.

And in this waking dream I don't name,

I bend in the moonlight. I let you screw me.

You are my incidental everything, Mori.

You are inside.

Obscenity is all we have now.

It is what we make with our lives.

Kiki takes the stolen shoes.

9: The tourist Fabian and Mori speak the same language

FABIAN: Gum?

MORI: What?

FABIAN: You want a stick? Juicy fruit.

MORI: Have we met?

FABIAN: There are many men like me.

MORI: ...Different shoes.

FABIAN: What?

MORI: Your shoes...they're not the same...

FABIAN: I wear sandals. It's hot.

MORI: I don't like sandals. I get blisters on my feet.

FABIAN: How unfortunate. You sure you don't -?

MORI: No. I like gum later.

FABIAN: After food?

MORI: After sex.

FABIAN: I prefer a cigarette.

MORI: I'm trying to quit. *[part of the façade]* Yeah. My dad, he died from it, cancer in the lungs. He smoked a lot. He smoked like five packs a day, but he didn't know, right? Cause the cigarettes were cheap. Cheaper than eats, than real food from the earth. I mean, cigarettes are from the earth, the tobacco is, but it's bad for you, right? It ruins you. I never liked him smoking. He stunk all the time. He was full of shadow. He had this red overcoat he would wear. Red overcoat and yellow face with yellow teeth. That was dad.

FABIAN: You remember things.

MORI: Dad, yeah, my papi, yeah. He was blood.

FABIAN: ...I like gum. It's a limited pleasure. You put it in your mouth, you chew, you wear it out, and then you toss it. It requires nothing of you.

MORI: It kills appetite.

FABIAN: Fuels it.

MORI: ...Where'd you get that?

FABIAN: The tie?

MORI: No, the other...

FABIAN: It's a pin. A Celtic dragon. My wife gave it to me. You didn't think?

MORI: What?

FABIAN: You didn't think I was married?

MORI: I don't think anything. I'm just here, right? I walk around, do stuff, go to the cybercafe.

FABIAN: You surf? There are some sites I could recommend. Travel and leisure. Education and sports. There are all kinds of options in life.

MORI: I eat fake food and pretend it's good. I hope the blank messages sent to my brain will stop. But they don't, right? They just keep going like sharks and shopping lists and cellphones and pigeons I try to scare off. There are so many damn pigeons. Where do they come from? They're mutants. They eat everything. Mceverything. They get fat. I watch them. I make them bleed. I take their skinny little breasts in my hands and suck them dry. You think I'm innocent? You think I have that kind of face? An innocent face? Screw you.

FABIAN: How much do you want?

MORI: What?

FABIAN: In what language

do you want me to speak?

[French] Combien voulez-vous?

{German] Wievel wunschen Sie?

[Italian] Quanto desiderate?

[Chinese] ...

[Spanish] Cuanto deseas?

...What's your name?

MORI: What do you care? I rim you and we're done with. This ain't no rela-tionship we're going to set up house and have kids and watch TV.

FABIAN: I'm Fabian.

MORI: You say your name like a Spaniard, like an Iberian...whatsit: "Fabian."

FABIAN: I say it how I was taught.

MORI: King Fabian went to the island,

King Fabian burnt his tongue

King Fabian let the cord move between his legs

All night long

King Fabian wanted to be a puppet

in Hansel and Gretel's show

King Fabian was tied up with strings

And given a starring role.

King Fabian wept and wept,

Until he could weep no more.

King Fabian stopped being a king

And let his puppet face glow

At night the children shunt him

By day the children laughed

At the sight of poor Fabian

Undone by the acrobat.

Poor Fabian, poor Fabian

Such a tale of woe

If only Fabian had relinquished his throne

He would still be standing. He would still be free

Instead of being a silly puppet

With a cord between his knees.

Poor Fabian, poor Fabian.

Such a tale of woe.

FABIAN: Where'd you learn that?

MORI: Grade school.

FABIAN: You made it up.

MORI: I make everything up. I'm Mori.

FABIAN: Mori?MORI: You don't like it? Call me something else.

FABIAN: Mori's fine.

10: Maura bereft of Mori

MAURA: Like smoke like a vacant moon he's gone for hours days endless time where where where and why has he gone without telling me, without a sign; It's not right; it's screwed-up alien abduction shit and he's going to pay okay? He is going to pay for this leaving me alone, cause I won't stand for it, I'm not one of those chicks that takes everything without asking, without question, not me. He's wrong about that. He wants to leave me? Fine. Leave, but don't come back. You hear me? I don't want to see you ever again loosy-goosy crybaby. I hope you rot. I hope you drown. I hope you're holed up in some well... I got wallets this time, Euro-man wallets and real live cash, my friend, and none of it is for you. You got that? Not a bit.

11: In the dark after sex spent

MORI: Angel honey baby.

FABIAN: Sweet words to one who will listen

MORI: Give me more

FABIAN: Why should I?

MORI: Cause I'm your Mori.

FABIAN: You have a weak tongue.

MORI: I drink and lick and spit and bite.

All for you.

FABIAN: And what will that get you?

MORI: Tokens for the arcade, a ride on the super-ski, a shoot-out in the cyber gun parade.

FABIAN: You act like a boy.

MORI: Does that mess you up, upset your equilibrium?

Fabian moves away.

MORI: Hey where are you- ? We've barely got going.

FABIAN: You have a weak tongue, Mori.

MORI: What are you talking about?

FABIAN: ...Who's Maura?

MORI: She's no one.

FABIAN: You screw me but you call out her name.

MORI: Angel honey, I got a lot of names in my head, baby.

FABIAN: Don't.

MORI: She's no one, all right? I swear.

FABIAN: ...You drink and sleep, and come.

MORI: I'm what you want, baby.

FABIAN: And cling like a rotten thing.

MORI: I am right inside, *papi.*

What do you want, baby? What do you need?

You want to screw all night? I can do it. Try me.

    Mori and Fabian begin to make love, then Fabian stops.

FABIAN: This is over.

MORI: Hey. Don't do that. We have an arrangement, no?

    Fabian gags Mori.

FABIAN: Let the whole world converge in your body and make ribbons inside you like a blood labyrinth.

And Fabian cuts Mori with a hidden knife.

12: While the cowboy of the islands hits the air

HILTON: We interrupt, we interrupt this program

To report an "incident in the Occident:"

In the broken alphabet of the spanking west

The capture and torture of dissidents

Is now allowed.

Rules change,

gravity shifts

And we are riding another wave now.

If you think things will change

Nothing will change.

That's the beauty of the Babel in which we live.

That's the killer of living in Troy,

as in the Troy who fell, and haunts us all.

In this miraculous Babylonia

Where miracles are what we count on now

trafficking bodies is part of the traffic we'll allow.

Hear my shout,

cowboys of the mini-isles,

Because the islands are vanishing in the Equi-tow

(in the toe of the liquid equator)

And He says "Okay!"

Huh?

"Okay!"

And we listen,

And bow.

13: Maura and Mori re-kick in slow time at the arcade, which used to be a bullring...

This begins as a wary, tentative reunion

MORI: In the speed shoot rush of the simulator surf

MAURA: And fighting off aliens

and ghouls all night

MORI: We shoot to kill

MAURA: We hack into all kinds of people's junk

MORI: Hitting the slots

MAURA: Raving to the beat

coming out of the disco speakers

MORI: Until we can't hear ourselves think

MAURA: Or speak

MORI: Just move

MAURA: And communicate with signs

They dance.

Hey

MORI: What?

MAURA: yeah

MORI: Okay

MAURA: Uh huh

MORI: Radical geniuses we are

MAURA: ...Tough moody and bad-ass

MORI: We think of nothing but

MAURA: Ourselves

MORI: And the orbit

MAURA: Our orbit

(establishing refrain) Hold on world

MORI: Hold on . . . . . .

And they are in sync.

MAURA: With *sangria* in our blood

MORI: Bleeding binary code

MAURA: Arcade hardware in our veins

MORI: Kick the slot

MAURA: Smash the screen with your hard fist

MORI: And never come down

MAURA: From this

From this

MORI: High.

MAURA: Delicious.

MORI: Delirious

MAURA: Mach ten.

MORI: Mach twenty.

MAURA: Mach maximum we rage and spin

Against the bankers and rodeo riders in our midst

Who walk with fear in their bellies

And old songs caught in their throats

MORI: We bury the old.

MAURA: We squash it

MORI: Hack it

MAURA: Steal it

MORI: Mix things up in the smog-choked city

MAURA: The silver city of stores where people buy nothing

MORI: Because no one can afford anything

MAURA: But themselves:

MORI: Human traffic.

MAURA: Trafficking in flesh, meat, and salsa.

Hold on world.

MORI: World.

Hold on . . . . . .

MAURA: Until we can't hold.

MORI: Until we can't spin

MAURA: Until we hate each other with so much passion

MORI: That we burn each other up.

MAURA: Crash-monsters.

MORI: Freaks of the millennial wave.

MAURA: Kill me, *sangron*. Do me in.

MORI: Disturbed I salivate and contemplate your extinction

MAURA: And I yours.

MORI: With pleasure.

MAURA: With what we're made of:

MORI: Junk skunk punk fury and misplaced velocity for a slow city

MAURA: Hit the slot.

MORI: Bang the token

MAURA: Eliminate me.

MORI: With pleasure.

MAURA: Eliminate me.

And we're inside each other like beasts

MORI: Monsters.

MAURA: Ready to rip

MORI: See through me.

MAURA: Blue wrap inner soul gimme

MORI: Skin

MAURA: Gimme

MORI: Marlboro-Inca pastiche

MAURA: nicotine cheap, you are.

MORI: I come as I am.

MAURA: Romper stomper

MORI: Arcade headliner.

MAURA: Yeah.

MORI: Yeah.

MAURA: Yeah.

MORI: And I'm through with you.

MAURA: I'm through...

MORI: Hold on world.

MAURA: Hold on . . . . . .

Don't leave me again.

You left and I was

MORI: Through. Yes.

MAURA: Pledge yourself to me

MORI: I pledge

MAURA: Burn

MORI: Every part of me

Every part of you

MAURA: And cut

Blood on blood. Cut me.

MORI: Now?

MAURA: We cut each other, our blood is one. Come on. Come on.

MORI: Hold on.

Hold . . . . . .

MAURA: And never leave.

Not now, not ever.

Swear.

Swear.

Mori.

MORI: And then in the cowboy funk

scratching my brain...

There's Kiki. What are you doing Kiki?

KIKI: Just kicking. You know me.

MORI: Where's the Milan guy?

KIKI: Out.

MORI: Did you give him a full frontal?

KIKI: He got some bebop feng shui, honey.

MAURA: Then why are you here? You should be in the chandelier room up at the Plaza-rific.

KIKI: Habit, honey.

MAURA: *Ritmo de lo habitual?*

KIKI: Yeah.

MAURA: This fetid bullring ain't your style.

KIKI: You are one dilated snarl.

MAURA: What of it?

KIKI: And Mori's out.

MORI: I'm speed racer, right? I'm not drinking Inca cola and farting crap.

KIKI: But where you've been, eh?

MORI: Here.

KIKI: Not here.

MAURA: He's through with that now. We've pledged to each other. Never to leave each other again.

KIKI: How very Romeo and Juliet.

MORI: Tristan and Isolde.

KIKI: The troops are out. On the street.

You shouldn't be here.

MAURA: We're from here. Not from some other where, but here. Right here.

MORI: You want to race a bit?

KIKI: I don't game.

MAURA: Then scoot, stop cramping me. Mori and I are going for an all-nighter.

KIKI: And then what?

MORI: And then another and another. We're making up, right? We're pledging our love.

KIKI: The troops will shoot through here, and won't stop. They don't believe in mercy.

MAURA: Let them. We'll take them on. We'll take everybody on. Bring out the knives. Come on. We'll show everyone what we're made of. How many people died here in the last twenty, thirty years? Nobody cares. It's just us, right? Getting by. They want our flesh? Come get it.

KIKI: You're crazy.

MAURA: I'm through and through. Not like you. A little snitch. Fine powder, the latest news... you are plugged in, aren't you? You are wired to the capitol. Are you turning us in, eh? Is that what this is? You're leading a squad here to tear down this place?

MORI: Kiki wouldn't do that.

KIKI: I should go.

MAURA: Why?

KIKI: I told you. I don't game.

MAURA: You stay. You got that? You stay here, you snitch.

KIKI: I'm stronger than you, honey. Don't mess with me.

MAURA: What are you going to do?

And Kiki tears into Maura with force

while Mori tries to intercede.

This is a fight of vengeance shot through with the sounds of the Old West distorted by Japanese anime.

Kiki and Maura duel, but Kiki is stronger.

As Kiki begins to choke Maura, Mori intercedes.

Kiki takes Mori on.

The music grows louder now from the old speakers.

Kiki begins to pummel Mori.

The electricity goes out in the swirling arcade.

And then slowly flares light up the sky.

And we see Mori in Maura's arms. His eyes are closed.

Nothing else. No one else for a long time.

Part Two

14: In daylight Mori sleeps outside;
the tourist now in another guise interrogates Mori

FABIAN: Name?

MORI: What?

FABIAN: Papers?

MORI: What?

FABIAN: Get up.

MORI: Don't kick me.

FABIAN: Sleeping is not allowed.

MORI: What?

FABIAN: Sleeping is prohibited.

MORI: What are you talking about?

FABIAN: Read the sign.

MORI: Hell.

FABIAN: No language.

MORI: Who the hell - ?

Fabian strikes Mori.

FABIAN: Name.

MORI: What?

FABIAN: Papers. No papers?

MORI: I'm getting them.

FABIAN: Where are you from?

MORI: Here.

FABIAN: Asylum?

MORI: What?

FABIAN: Is that why you're here? For asylum?

MORI: Do I know you?

FABIAN: Keep your spine straight.

MORI: I know you. Your voice is familiar.

FABIAN: Straight.

MORI: Hey, come on, baby-

Fabian strikes Mori.

FABIAN: Don't initiate. Only what I ask. Understand?

MORI: ...Yes.

FABIAN: Where are you from?

What's your language?

Papers?

Name?

...

Repeat after me. A.

MORI: A.

FABIAN: Ass.

MORI: Ass.

Fabian strikes Mori

FABIAN: No language. Rules.

B. Repeat.

MORI: B.

FABIAN: Bull-crap.

MORI: What?

FABIAN: Repeat.

MORI: Bull-crap.

Fabian strikes Mori.

FABIAN: C. Repeat. Repeat.

MORI: ...No...

Fabian strikes Mori

FABIAN: Repeat.

MORI: ...I won't...

Fabian strikes Mori

FABIAN: Word only. Word C. Repeat.

...

No memory?

MORI: ...Yes.

FABIAN: Here is a list of what you want. Read. Can you read?

MORI: Yes.

FABIAN: ...Out loud.

MORI: I want...

FABIAN: Louder.

MORI: I want to die.

FABIAN: ...Continue.

MORI: I want to regret.

FABIAN: Louder.

MORI: I want to change

FABIAN: Louder.

MORI: I want to leave.

I want to hate.

I want to cry.

I want to forget.

FABIAN: Repeat. Louder.

MORI: I want to forget.

FABIAN: ...Sign.

Mori pisses on the piece of paper.

Lick it. Lick your signature.

MORI: No.

FABIAN: You refuse?

MORI: ...I refuse everything.

FABIAN: ...You are number 015125. You will answer to this number and this number only. You are now a female, understand? A girl. No trace.

MORI: What?

FABIAN: You have no memory.

Fabian blindfolds Mori, and drags him away.

15: Hilton croons a country bolero
like a true cowboy
against the radio static

"Goodbye song"

HILTON: Today I know you left me

Today I wave goodbye

How sad, how cruel, how lonely

Is life on this isle.

Oh please say you will remember

That once I passed you by

In favor of a stranger

Who had danger in his eyes

In favor of a lover,

In whose eyes I admired mine.

[spoken] And this is radio *Dos Equis*

saying good night

On this long night turned day

There is silence on the street

After yesterday's riots.

No one was left standing at the factory,

at the arcade,

at the old radio museum...

There is only silence now.

Limited freedom.

And tequila ice cubes on our tongues

To make us slowly

dis-remember.

16. Kiki and Maura see each other

KIKI: No Mori?

MAURA: Don't talk to me.

KIKI: I'm sorry.

MAURA: No words.

KIKI: I'm sorry. Bruises.The fight... before. I didn't mean -

MAURA: We were sleeping. He was sleeping. We were quiet. Perfect citizens, right? No sound, no mess. Just sleep, being close. Close tight with each other. I got up. I was awake. I was coming down from all... mess in my head, heart pumping, pulse going, weird coming down. I needed to walk about. Streets empty. Yeah. People hiding. Sound of gun-shots every once in a while. Dead dogs, whacked-out canaries... zoo, right? Like a death zoo. And I'm walking. Not far. Just to move. I need to move my legs. I need to get about. "I'll be back in a sec, Mori." But I get lost. That's the truth. I couldn't remember what street I was on. Everything was too quiet. I was spooked. Didn't know myself. I couldn't even move. Like everything was caving in. Piece of trash in my stomach. Ache, right? Fake bits of food sticking in me. I feel like gagging. Like vomiting up everything. But I can't. I don't know where I am. Red shutters on a door of a building. There's a sign up. It says "Sunday House." I'm thinking "church, right?" But it's not. It's an ice-cream place. They've spelt the word wrong. They don't know the language right. One scoop for a dollar. I get close. And then the street turns. I swear it just turned. And I could see the sea, and a pelican nibbling on a discarded CD. The pelican was looking for some nourishment. All the real food here goes elsewhere. Even gunk, the good gunk, the fine effing blow goes elsewhere. And I'm staring at the picture of an ice cream sundae. And I suddenly know where I am. I'm next street over. Near the bodega, and the tourist trap hotel, And I think "Mori, I'll be right there." And I'm quick heart-stopping running to where I left him, to where we lay, and he's gone. No trace.

KIKI: ...I thought I saw him.

MAURA: When?

KIKI: With a guy.

MAURA: What guy?

KIKI: I don't know. It might not have been him.

MAURA: Don't do that. Don't go silent on me, Kiki. Come on, snitch. Spill.

KIKI: Look, honey, I'm not good at details. He was with a guy. That's all I know.

They exchanged something.

MAURA: What?

KIKI: Papers.

MAURA: What kind of papers? Newspapers?

KIKI: No. Smaller. Like at the doctor's, you know.

MAURA: Prescription?

KIKI: Yeah. Yeah, honey. Prescription. Must have been. And then they walked away.

MAURA: Don't lie to me. You lie to me, I'll kill you.

KIKI: You really love him, eh?

MAURA: He's my life.

KIKI: No one should be your life.

MAURA: Well, he is. He's always has been.

KIKI: Was this before or after you came from *Vayazul*?

MAURA: *Vayazul, agua azul*, what the crap is it to you? Mori and I are mates. We're like blood. We speak the same language. He's my life, yeah. Now, which way did they go?

KIKI: That way I think. Towards the old hospital, towards the sea.

MAURA: Here.

KIKI: What's this?

MAURA: Euro-wallet.

KIKI: What about you? Hey, Maura. Crazy girl...

Kiki is left with the wallet. Maura runs away.

17: As Mori writes a letter to Maura in silence

MORI: They stole my tongue, Maura.

They took it just like that,

and I didn't even have a chance to...

I hear things. I smell things. Salt and piss.

I hear waves. I must be near the sea.

They took me, Maura.

They stole my name. They took it from me.

They took my sex, too.

They say I'm a girl. They want me to believe this.

I have to act like one. For them.

For people that seem so familiar,

And yet I don't know where they're from.

Lights out. All dark.

Sometimes the light never comes... not for days.

I hear waves and think of the sea.

Some people say in dreams

things get taken from you.

But I don't sleep. I never sleep.

My eyes are pressed open now.

I miss my tongue, Maura.

I miss the virtual jet-ski.

I miss standing in front of the deep peep

and screwing for eternity.

I hear you, Maura. I hear you cursing at the sea.

I want to die.

I want to regret.

I want to change.

I want to leave.

I want to hate.

I want to cry.

I want to dream.

The night falls in waves.

The earth shifts.

The arcade is far away and Maura picks up a voice in the air.

It is Mori's voice. The cowboy of the islands, of the airwaves, sleeps,

As Maura makes her way through the brush, while Kiki sings an old song to anyone who will listen.

"A city by the sea"

KIKI: There's a city on the ocean.

Give me another drink and you'll see.

Silent waves are breaking

Everything will be released.

Go on, fish, sleep.

Go on, fish, dream.

There's a city on the ocean.

Give me another drink and you'll see.

Quiet waves are breaking.

Everything will be released.

Go on, fish, sleep.

Go on, fish, dream

Go on, fish, sleep.

Go on -

A single loud military sound cuts off the song,

followed by a long silence.

18. In simultaneous frames

HILTON (on the radio)

All is quiet

We are happy

FABIAN'S VOICE: Number 015125

HILTON: We are stabilized

FABIAN'S VOICE: Report to room twenty

HILTON: The alphabet gleams

FABIAN'S VOICE: For lesson one hundred and three

HILTON: It is bankrupt.

MORI'S VOICE: Number 015125 reporting.

HILTON: It is complete.

Mori appears in the empty room. He wears dress and heels. No makeup.

HILTON: Our language is one of perfect

FABIAN'S VOICE: Move now. Move like a girl.

HILTON: Equilibrium.

Mori moves across the room as a girl would.

No more malas noches

FABIAN'S VOICE: More feminine, please.

HILTON: No more waking at four a.m.

FABIAN'S VOICE: And dance.

HILTON: To strange sounds.

Kiki, in distance, sings softly chorus from "A city by the sea."

Everything is normal now.

We move in unison.

Kiki, in distance, sings...

All difference

Is erased.

FABIAN'S VOICE: More movement

In the hips. Yes.

HILTON: The city lifts its smog

FABIAN'S VOICE: And keep dancing.

HILTON: To welcome piracy of all kinds

FABIAN'S VOICE: Wilder. Yes.

HILTON: Branded goods are produced

FABIAN'S VOICE: Like a hungry girl.

HILTON: In mass quantities

FABIAN'S VOICE: Like a starving girl.

HILTON: More than before. More than ever.

We allow our language to be owned

FABIAN'S VOICE: Full of lust and desire.

HILTON: To be protected

FABIAN'S VOICE: Feel your breasts.

HILTON: To be copyrighted.

FABIAN'S VOICE: Feel your thighs.

HILTON: This is how we live after Babel,

FABIAN'S VOICE: Between your thighs.

Gyrate. Thrust your pelvis.

HILTON: After the sleek angels of history

Have let down their guard.

FABIAN'S VOICE: Improvise. Like a girl.

HILTON: Hold on, world.

FABIAN'S VOICE: Always.

HILTON: Hold on.

18a) after the simultaneous frames, it's just the room

FABIAN'S VOICE: ...

And strip.

Mori pauses.

Like a girl.

You must strip.

...

Number 015125, are you listening to me?

MORI: Yes.

FABIAN'S VOICE: No words, please.

Just the body. Just a sign.

And strip.

Mori begins to strip.

Slowly. Slowly. Like a girl.

Very shy. Very modest.

A virtuous girl filled with shame.

As Mori strips very slowly,

Maura is seen in another place.

She is transforming herself into a boy.

Mori speaks to Maura as if he can see her.

MORI: Maura? What are you doing?

MAURA: Shh... Don't tell.

MORI: Are you changing yourself for me?

MAURA: I'm heading to the country, to the open fields. Do you see me?

MORI: Maura?

FABIAN'S VOICE: No words. No voice. Just a body, please.

MORI: I'm a girl now. That's what they tell me. I am a number.

I am shut inside this place.

Find me.

FABIAN'S VOICE: Quiet.

MORI: I'm a criminal. I'ma number. Find me.

FABIAN'S VOICE: Quiet.

MORI: Maura?

MAURA: I will.

FABIAN'S VOICE: Silence!

Mori is naked. Maura is now disguised transformed.

Fabian appears.

FABIAN: Number 015125, you have failed lesson one hundred and three.

Open your mouth, please.

Leave it open.

Do not cover yourself.

Do not try to leave.

In the distance, Maura runs away.

MORI: Maura?

FABIAN: Number 015125. Are you number 015125?

MORI: Yes.

FABIAN: Repeat.

MORI: 015125.

FABIAN: Your crimes?

MORI: None.

FABIAN: Crimes against state and nature. Repeat.

MORI: No.

FABIAN: Crimes against state and nature.

...

Lie down please.

Lie down.

And mouth open. Wide.

Keep open.

Fabian kicks Mori in the mouth..

19: Kiki calls to a passer-by

KIKI: Everybody's leaving.

They hide or escape

or throw themselves to the sea.

Except me.

I don't leave. I like the city.

Honey, come closer. Be rough.

Come on. I can take.

My body can take anything.

You're sweet. You're candy. Eh?

You buy me some toothpaste, honey?

You buy me some gum?

Toilet paper, condoms, some ecstasy?

I can take. I take everything.

I stock up now. Cause there's nothing.

You hear me?

Don't leave.

I'll be your baby. I will.

Rub me. Yeah. I won't bite. You see?

I'm Kiki. I'm Gloria. I'm everything.

And when the guards come

in the name of freedom,

and they'll come, cause they always do

In this *carajo* country

I won't say anything. I'll be a good quiet one.

I keep the best secrets.

You see that old hospital over there

out by the fields?

It hasn't been a hospital in years.

You don't believe me?

Believe what you want.

What does it matter, eh?

We'll all be dead soon.

20: Maura in disguise asks a man from the fields about Mori

The man has a rifle in hand.

FRANKIE: *Aqui no hay nadie.*

MAURA: Speak English.

FRANKIE: No one here. Who you look for?

MAURA: My brother.

FRANKIE: *Que chulo.*

MAURA: Quit.

FRANKIE: You don't like my hands, boy?

MAURA: Did you see him or not?

FRANKIE: That's not how you find someone. By asking just like that.

A moment.

MAURA: How then?

FRANKIE: ...See? You need me.

MAURA: I don't need anyone.

FRANKIE: Don't be a *tirano*.

MAURA: Speak English.

FRANKIE: Why?

MAURA: I don't want to hear anything else.

FRANKIE: What kind of English do you want me to speak? There are so many kinds.

MAURA: Speak what I can understand, *cabron*.

FRANKIE: You speak Spanish, eh?

MAURA: I speak words. Where is he?

FRANKIE: You are too direct. You will never find him with such directness.

MAURA: I came all the way out here, didn't I? I found my way here.

FRANKIE: He is your brother?

MAURA: Yes. (*A moment.*) He's my lover.

FRANKIE: One boy to another?

MAURA: Yes.

FRANKIE: I sensed this.

MAURA: You get no brownie points from me.

FRANKIE: What is that? Brownie points? What is that, eh?

MAURA: An expression.

FRANKIE: What does it mean, boy?

MAURA: It's an American expression.

FRANKIE: Is it a good thing?

MAURA: I think so.

FRANKIE: Okay. ...And you, you're not American?

MAURA: I'm nothing.

FRANKIE: No one's nothing.

MAURA: I am nothing. I am a mutt.

No breeding. No stock. No line. Nothing. There's no geography to me.

FRANKIE: *Que pena.*

MAURA: Speak English.

FRANKIE: A shame for you to be nothing, to feel nothing. Except for him? You feel for him?

MAURA: Have you seen him?

FRANKIE: I could have seen something. This photo you show me is not very good.

MAURA: It's from a booth.

FRANKIE: What's that?

MAURA: You go in, you get your photo taken, it comes out of the machine.

FRANKIE: A city thing?

MAURA: An American thing.

FRANKIE: Well, it's not a good photo. But you know him a long time, yes?

MAURA: Long enough.

FRANKIE: I have a romantic nature. I do. I understand these things. Wanting to see the lover, wanting to possess the beloved. But if he leaves of his own accord, there is nothing you can do. No one to find where there's no one. You see? The hospital is abandoned. There hasn't been anyone there for years.

MAURA: How do you know?

FRANKIE: I live here. I was born here and I'll die here. I know things. I'm witness.

MAURA: To what?

FRANKIE: To time passing. Nothing else. You have *papeles*?

MAURA: Speak English.

FRANKIE: Papers?!

MAURA: I have ID. Yeah.

FRANKIE: Let's see.

MAURA: Is this what you do?

FRANKIE: I guard this road. Yes. That is my job. That is one of my jobs.

MAURA: What's the other?

FRANKIE: I move things from one place to the next. I move markers, burial places. I establish order. I do not question. I just act, do. I keep things where they need to be, where they should be. I could help you. I am tender-hearted. Don't I look tender-hearted?

MAURA: You look how you look.

FRANKIE: And you look how you want.

MAURA: What do you mean?

FRANKIE: Are you a boy?

MAURA: Yes.

FRANKIE: For how long?

MAURA: Since the day I was born.

FRANKIE: Punch me.

She punches him.

Harder.

She punches him again.

You have strength.

MAURA: I box.

FRANKIE: In a ring?

MAURA: Outside in the park, on the street...

FRANKIE: You're a sweet boy. Is this your ID?

Mauro?

MAURA: Yes.

FRANKIE: Unusual.

MAURA: It's not common.

FRANKIE: I'm Frankie. I'm very common.

MAURA: You through with my ID?

FRANKIE: It's nothing to me. Call yourself what you like. Mauro's as good a name as any.

MAURA: You don't believe me? I have a tattoo.

FRANKIE: No need to show. I believe.

MAURA: Why?

FRANKIE: Because you want me to.

MAURA: You're a stupid man.

FRANKIE: And you're a sweet boy, but you know nothing. Y'hear me? There are screams, and children on fire. Sweet children walking in flames. Even here far from the city. Don't look away from me, Mauro. Keep your eyes on me, or I shoot you right now!...What does he mean to you, Mauro? What does this boy in the photo mean to you?

MAURA: I told you.

FRANKIE: You said he was your lover. That's not enough.

MAURA: What do you want from me?

FRANKIE: Some feeling, Mauro. Not enough these days. Everyone is closed up, shut down, hiding, afraid, and in the end, they are taken away anyway. Understand?

MAURA: ...Mori and I...

FRANKIE: Yes?

MAURA: We kick and shout...

FRANKIE: Go on.

MAURA: And dance and hang, and think of nothing and think of everything...

FRANKIE: Why you get quiet, eh? I asked for some feeling. Give.

MAURA: We go inside each other.

FRANKIE: *Asi.*

MAURA: And we drown the world and forget and dream and not dream and kick again and we don't even think about it.

FRANKIE: *Con ganas.* Yeah.

MAURA: We just wiggle and waste cause there's nothing else, right? Just waking and falling back to sleep on the inside of the inside, on the flip side of ecstasy, static blinking and not thinking about another day cause it doesn't matter, nothing matters in this state. Just us. Only us. Mori and Mauro. Mauro and Mori joined at the hip no matter what... We know this. We think the same. We feel the same. He is my tongue. And I am his body. You see? We are joined. We are one being. Is that what you want? Is that what you need? Is this enough for you, mister Frankie?

Frankie punches her.

FRANKIE: The sky was powder gray. Full of bursts. I was ten years old. I was at an air show. Everything was loud. I wanted to be a pilot. My papi held me. He said "Look up, son. Don't cover your ears. Take it all in." And I did. I pointed up at each plane. I shouted. I made a scene. "Who's that little boy? Why doesn't he behave?" I didn't know what that was. I was my father's son. The fireworks happened at the end of the show. We were on the grounds. Cars were parked for miles. We sat on the hood of a car that wasn't ours and watched the greens and reds shoot up into the sky one after the other. I tried to hold my *papi*'s hand, but he couldn't see me. So, we sat letting the smoke from the fireworks sting our eyes, burst upon burst. I thought "This is how it will always be between us: *Papi* looking up, caught in something, dreaming, and me, wanting a touch, a bit of acknowledgment, and never getting anything."...I put my hand inside you. We take our time. You walk away.

MAURA: And what do I get?

FRANKIE: There's a path. I know it well. I show it to you.

Maura begins to undress.

FRANKIE: What's the hurry?

MAURA: I don't have time.

21: Mori and Maura share a dream

Feel my hand?

Through the wall?

Yes.

Can you hear me?

A little.

Where are you now?

On the path.

In the dark?

Yes.

Your voice is funny.

So is yours. Why don't you curse at me?

I don't want to. I'm a boy now.

Better yet. Better reason to.

Your voice is still funny.

My mouth is broken. This has been done to protect me, to stop me from speaking. I write words in the air. I send messages as if on a screen like in the cyber. Do you hear me?

I always hear you.

...Where's Kiki?

Is she with you?

Is he?

Who?

The tourist.

How do you know about him?

I know everything. We are joined, remember?

...I'm closer now. I'm a boy. We are the same.

You're not a boy. You never will be.

You're not strong enough.

I'm stronger than you.

You miss me.

I hold you. Yes. I reach out my hand through the wall where they hold me, where they keep me.

Can you see me?

I am blind.

No eyes? No mouth?

Everything is dark. My tongue spits Z's.

Z.

The end of the alphabet.

Crave me.

Want me.

In some countries there is no want.

In some countries there is no need...of anything.

I get hit every day. I hit everyone back. My fists break walls.

...Closer?

Yes.

I feel your breath.

In what room do they keep you?

Is it because of me?

Is that why they have taken you?

Because of me? Because of my family?

Because of *Vayazul* and aristocracy?

They take because they take, because they can. I am a refugee.

You were born here.

Only you know this. But to them....

...You're very faint.

My voice goes. It will come back soon.

Mori?

Maura.

You're far away, far from me.

The walls tremble.

(unison) I punch, I kick. I will not lose faith.

In the ocean...

Yes.

There's graffiti.

What does it say?

I can't make it out.

Try.

Salt words in a salt sea.

Read them.

[French] Une nouvelle langue,

[Portuguese] uma lingua nova,

[German] eine neue Sprache

A new language

Your voice is clear.

My accent's crap. I learned the wrong alphabet.

I want to see you close.

With blind eyes?

With every part of me.

...I'm here now. Our fingers touch.

Die.

Regret.

Change.

Leave.

Hate.

Cry.

Forget.

Love.

22: Awake in real time, Maura encounters Mori who has been tossed out onto a bone heap.

MAURA: Mori?

MORI: 015125.

MAURA: It's me. Remember?

MORI: You're a boy.

MAURA: I'm pretending. But I'm not. See?

MORI: It's wrong to pretend. Lesson two: do not pretend you are anything.

MAURA: Okay.

MORI: Bones here. Dead. The dead are here. Arms and legs. Smashed skulls. I am dead too.

MAURA: Mori?

MORI: What a stupid name. Whose name is that? Yours?

MAURA: It's yours. Remember?

MORI: I am 015125. I was born in another country. I am a girl, age twenty. I am dead.

Stop looking at me.

MAURA: You're bruised.

MORI: I have broken things inside. Outside, I have marks. I am disposable. Trash. I wait now for crows, gulls. For my flesh to be picked, for another number maybe.

MAURA: Come here.

MORI: You have cold hands. Like wax.

MAURA: You need to get out of here.

MORI: Lesson number one thousand and two: do not leave, do not try to leave, never leave, or much drowning, head in bucket, pulling of limbs.

MAURA: I'll carry you.

MORI: Don't touch me. Please.

MAURA: Okay.

MORI: You speak funny.

MAURA: I speak how I speak.

MORI: You have an accent. Lesson five: no accents.

MAURA: Is that what you've been taught?

MORI: No questions. Repeat.

MAURA: What?

MORI: Repeat.

MAURA...This man put his hands on me. I let him. I'd do anything. And there was another man after that, and another. All along the road. Men waiting. Men with dogs. Sad men doing their job of guarding. I walked the whole way. I became rougher and rougher outside, and more and more gentle inside. I would cry at weird times. In the middle of sex. In the middle of trade. At no hour, no anything. A tear would come. And another. And music was so distant. I thought there was a disco on one side of the road but it was just an abandoned radio playing inside an empty house stained with fresh blood. I kept walking. The last man along the road was right. There was a path. Not too far. A possible path. A visible path. ...I wanted to be back at the arcade. I wanted noise and lots of noise. Beeps, pops, shots, bells, mechanical cheers from a screen crowd. Reactivate. Reload. Start again.

MORI: Beeps and pops?

MAURA: From a machine. Alpine Ski. Speed Racer. Remember?

MORI: Rush...

MAURA: Yes. Yes. Speed shoot rush. Remember?

MORI: ...I listen to the sea. This leg I think was from number 017127. A young man. Very tall. No eyes. I listen to the sea.

MAURA: Mori?

MORI: Forget me.

MAURA: Mori?

MORI: Erase memory.

MAURA: ...I'll stay here with you. Yes?

MORI: You're a strange boy.

MAURA: Yes.

MORI: We listen to the sea.

MAURA: Yes.

Mori and Maura look at the ocean.

23: The cowboy's voice hits the quiet air

HILTON: In the A, B, D and number four

We come to you live from the capital city

Where the new voice of freedom

can be heard for miles,

and the electric boogaloo gives way

To a synthetic *merengue*

conveniently lifted off an old laptop.

Two pure ones

have been found

hard as mules

on the sand

against the rough sea,

they are seenwe are told

through a night of lucid silver.

Kiki in view...

KIKI: What will you do with your hands?

What will you dream with your eyes?

HILTON: Two walls

silent as a rose

KIKI: cast their double shadow

at break of dawn.

HILTON: Two pure bodies

KIKI: lean as mules

HILTON: were found

KIKI: bound to each other

on the sand.

HILTON: But nobody dares untie

this Mori,

KIKI: this Maura

HILTON: who in one motion

gave themselves up to the moon.

Against the sea wall, Mori and Maura are found.

They are nude. They are entwined.

End of play

WRECKAGE

(after Euripides' *Medea*)

by

CARIDAD SVICH

Script history:

This script was written on a residency from the Inge Center for the Arts in Kansas.

Subsequently the play received a rehearsed reading at New Dramatists in New York under the direction of Annie Dorsen. The cast was comprised of Florencia Lozano (Woman), David Barlow (First Son), Greg Steinbruner (Second Son), Ron Riley (Nurse), and Michael Gladis (Husband).

A revised draft of the script received a mini-workshop at New Dramatists as part of the PlayTime Studio for New Plays under the direction of Stefan Novinski. The cast was comprised of Florencia Lozano (Woman), Alfredo Narciso (First Son), Aaron Yoo (Second Son), Chris Wells (Nurse) and Keith Randolph Smith (Husband). Dramaturgs: Liz Duffy Adams and David Grimm.

It also received a workshop at The Hartt School/University of Hartford as part of their New Play Festival, and development with Highwire Theatre's Testing the Line reading series in NYC under Adriana Baer's direction.

The play received its world premiere with Crowded Fire Theatre in San Francisco, CA at the Boxcar Playhouse on May 9, 2009. It was directed by Erin Gilley; the set design was by Evren Odcikin; the costume design was by Bree Hylkema; lighting design by Tim Szostek; video design by Wesley Cabral; sound design by Marc Blinder; and original songs composed by Caridad Svich. Mollie Flanagan was the stage manager, Elana McKernan was the assistant director, and Sonia Fernandez was the dramaturg. Artistic Director of Crowded Fire Theatre : Marissa Wolf. The cast was as follows:

First Son . . . . . . Eric Kerr

Second Son . . . . . . Detroit Dunwood

Woman . . . . . . Laura Jane Cole

Husband . . . . . . David Sinaiko

Nurse . . . . . . Lawrence Radecker

Broadcast (VO . . . . . . Paul Lancour

The play received its midwest premiere with Caffeine Theatre in Chicago, IL at Stage 773 Theatre on March 11, 2011. It was directed by Joanie Schultz; the set design was by Stephen Carmody; the costume design was by Alarie Hammock; lighting design by Casey Diers*; projection & video design by Davonte Johnson; sound design by Thomas Dixon; and original songs composed by Caridad Svich. Rose Streit was the stage manager, Cody Estle was the assistant director, and Dan Smith was the dramaturg. Technical Director was Eric Sisco. Artistic Director (Interim) of Caffeine Theatre : Meghan Beals McCarthy. The cast was as follows:

Woman . . . . . . DANA BLACK*

First Son . . . . . . TIM MARTIN

Second Son . . . . . . IAN DANIEL McLAREN

Nurse . . . . . . SEAN THOMAS

Husband . . . . . . JEREMY VAN METER*

Understudy . . . . . . ERIK SCHNITGER*

*Caffeine Theatre Artistic Associate

This work is inspired, in part, by Jeff Buckley's cover version of Hank Williams' song "Lost Highway."

Roles:

FIRST SON, homeless, slightly brooding, sensitive, passionate, wary.

SECOND SON, homeless, open, fluid, androgynous.

WOMAN, 30s-40s, fierce, attractive, sensual, elegant

NURSE, played by male. 40s-50s, slightly off-kilter, darkly humorous, honest, somewhat prescient.

HUSBAND, 30s-40s, strong, powerful, contained, and caustic

BROADCAST (VO), the clear, emotionally detached voice on the airwaves, male.

Places:

The private beach, the gleaming house, the road, the boardwalk, and the convenience store of the jeweled city along the isthmus.

Note:

Melodies to original song fragments in the text may be obtained by contacting the author, or the lyrics may be re-set by another composer.

1.

Waves. White hot sun. A cold beach. A distant broadcast is heard midst the waves.

(VO): The bodies of two boys were found yesterday morning. They were re-trieved from the sea at about 9 AM. Both boys had been struck with a blunt object, but otherwise, outside of a little blood, their bodies showed no other significant signs of violence. It is not known how long they were in the water, or who is responsible for their deaths.

Waves. Two boys are seen on the beach, blood-marked in beauty. They are draped across each other, eyes closed, entwined. They wear simple street clothes and are barefoot. They awaken slowly, and stare at the water.

A surveillance camera at a convenience store near the site recorded the last known appearance of the boys, who are believed to be brothers. Circumstances surrounding the deaths are unknown, although both boys are said to have been wearing vaguely feminine attire when they were found. In other news, the weather report promises highs in the low 80s, perfect for a day at the beach.

Silence.

SECOND SON: Was it like this?

FIRST SON: What?

SECOND SON: Swimming?

FIRST SON: Don't know.

SECOND SON: Don't you remember?

FIRST SON: I don't remember anything.

SECOND SON: Not even me?

FIRST SON: Of course I remember you. You're here.

SECOND SON: I remember a kiss. A woman's lips on my hands. Very sweet.

FIRST SON: When was this?

SECOND SON: I don't know. Not long ago.

FIRST SON: You're dreaming.

SECOND SON: No. This is what I remember.

FIRST SON: Well, I don't recall anyone kissing you.

SECOND SON: That's because you don't recall anything.

FIRST SON: A woman?

SECOND SON: Yes.

FIRST SON: What was she like?

SECOND SON: Tall. Strong. Pretty. She had tears in her eyes.

FIRST SON: How come?

SECOND SON: She was angry.

FIRST SON: Not mournful?

SECOND SON: No. Not grieving. She was furious, and sweet at the same time. Don't you remember?

FIRST SON: No.

SECOND SON: She held me.

FIRST SON: A cuddle?

SECOND SON: More than that. An embrace.

FIRST SON: Full on?

SECOND SON: Very warm. Very tender. I think she loved me.

FIRST SON: You're making it up.

SECOND SON: I'm not.

FIRST SON: Some woman held you?

SECOND SON: I was in her arms for a long time.

FIRST SON: And then?

SECOND SON: She kissed me.

FIRST SON: A kiss is important. A kiss is everything sometimes.

Pause.

SECOND SON: Do you want to?

FIRST SON: What?

SECOND SON: Kiss.

FIRST SON: Somebody might see.

SECOND SON: There's no one here.

FIRST SON: Might be. You don't know.

SECOND SON: What of it?

FIRST SON: You don't know how to kiss. You've no practice.

SECOND SON: I remember.

FIRST SON: A woman's lips on your hand? That's not a real kiss.

SECOND SON: What'd you mean?

FIRST SON: Hands don't count. Lips are what do.

SECOND SON: Who said?

...You don't want me to kiss you.

FIRST SON: I didn't say that.

SECOND SON: You're shy.

FIRST SON: I'm not. Never have been. I'm not remotely shy.

SECOND SON: You don't act it.

FIRST SON: Kiss me. Go on. But not on my hands. I want a real kiss, yeah. Tongue and everything.

Second Son kisses First Son lightly. Pause.

SECOND SON: Well?

FIRST SON: I don't know.

SECOND SON: Did it feel like anything?

FIRST SON: It was all right.

SECOND SON: That's all?

FIRST SON: It was fine. What'd you want?

You want to be reciprocated for your affection?

SECOND SON: What are you talking about?

FIRST SON: Words, right? I remember. They're in my brain. Tons of them waiting to be let out. "Affection" is a fine word.

Pause. First Son kisses Second Son. Pause.

Aren't you going to say anything?

SECOND SON: You bit me. I've got blood...

FIRST SON: I didn't mean...

SECOND SON: It was nice. I liked it.

FIRST SON: Want another?

SECOND SON: No. I'm fine.

Pause.

FIRST SON: I can't tell what you are.

SECOND SON: Sorry?

FIRST SON: You're familiar to me.

SECOND SON: So are you.

FIRST SON: But I can't...

SECOND SON: Split somehow...

FIRST SON: Yes. My memory's split. That's a good word. "Split." It's perfect, really.

Sounds exactly like what it means.

Look at you.

SECOND SON: What?

FIRST SON: You look like everything.

SECOND SON: What'd you mean?

FIRST SON: Beauteous. *[from memory]* "Beauteous babe, you have a city, where far from me and my sad lot you will live."

SECOND SON: What are you going on about?

FIRST SON: Words. Figments. Fragments.

SECOND SON: You're funny.

FIRST SON: *[from memory]* "Behold my lover's laughing eyes."

SECOND SON: I'm not your lover.

FIRST SON: Aren't you?

SECOND SON: I don't think so.

FIRST SON: What, then?

Second Son heads to the water.

SECOND SON: Come on, silly. Let's go for a swim.

FIRST SON: No.

SECOND SON: Just for a bit.

FIRST SON: I'm not going in.

SECOND SON: Are you afraid?

FIRST SON: No.

SECOND SON: Then why not?

FIRST SON: I don't like the sea.

SECOND SON: But we're here. Look at it. Isn't it just...?

FIRST SON: Yes. It is.

SECOND SON: But you still won't...?

FIRST SON: No.

SECOND SON: I'd like to go in.

FIRST SON: Go on, then.

SECOND SON: Will you watch me?

FIRST SON: Why should I?

SECOND SON: You're older than me.

FIRST SON: So?

SECOND SON: So, you're supposed to take care of me. Older boys take care of younger boys.

FIRST SON: Are you a younger boy?

SECOND SON: Of course. Don't I look it?

FIRST SON: I suppose.

SECOND SON: Well, you're older. That's clear.

FIRST SON: I'm not old.

SECOND SON: No, but you're older. Definitely. So, you've got a duty.

FIRST SON: To take care?

SECOND SON: That's the law.

FIRST SON: Since when?

SECOND SON: Always.

FIRST SON: That's a burden.

SECOND SON: Look, are you going to watch me or not?

FIRST SON: All right.

SECOND SON: Swear.

FIRST SON: You're so serious for such a young boy.

SECOND SON: Promise.

Second Son extends his hand to First Son.

FIRST SON: *[taking his hand]* ...I do.

SECOND SON: ...I'm going in. Straight into the sea. Watch me. (*They let go of each other. Second Son walks away.*) Are you watching?

FIRST SON: Yes.

SECOND SON: Are you watching?

FIRST SON: Yes.

Second son goes into the water. Pause. First son looks away.

2.

Some time passes. First Son rests on the sand. A Woman dressed in ultra-chic evening-wear approaches. She carves space and time as she walks. She regards the First Son.

WOMAN: Well, look at you.

FIRST SON: I fell asleep.

WOMAN: I know. I watched you. You have soft eyelids.

FIRST SON: Do I?

WOMAN: Like a child. A beauteous babe.

FIRST SON: Hmm?

WOMAN: Isn't that your name?

FIRST SON: No.

WOMAN: I could've sworn...

FIRST SON: Not beauteous. Not babe. I'm just me. The first.

WOMAN: I can't call you that.

FIRST SON: Call me what you like, then.

WOMAN: Lost?

FIRST SON: I'm not. I know exactly where I am.

WOMAN: Where are you?

FIRST SON: Beach. White shimmering sand. Tit cold, but sun hot. And you're dressed for the evening. Am I right?

WOMAN: Quite right.

FIRST SON: First of firsts. That's me. First to get everything. First to get hit, first to get kissed. Sure of my stride.

WOMAN: And the younger?

FIRST SON: What?

WOMAN: Have you forgotten him already? There was a younger boy here too.

FIRST SON: When was this?

WOMAN: Don't lie to me. I saw him.

FIRST SON: He went for a swim.

WOMAN: And then?

FIRST SON: He went away. To the city, I think. He was hungry.

WOMAN: Young boys are always hungry.

FIRST SON: That they are.

WOMAN: Are you a boy?

FIRST SON: Of course.

WOMAN: You don't look it. Not at first glance.

FIRST SON: Do you mind?

WOMAN: I don't mind anything.

FIRST SON: I wish I could be like that. Un-mindful of things. I try. But I get tired somehow. The waves come up fierce-like. After a while, I can't look at them. All these words come into my head. And I have to close my eyes.

WOMAN: What kind of words?

FIRST SON: Hapless ruinous words. Fragrant and sweet upon the breath, but full of sorrow

WOMAN: You shouldn't be here.

FIRST SON: I'll go.

He starts to walk away. She pulls him back.

WOMAN: Where are you going to go? You're nothing without me.

FIRST SON: I don't understand.

WOMAN: Somebody's got to watch me.

FIRST SON: Why?

WOMAN: I might do something awful. And then where would we be?

FIRST SON: Heaven.

Pause.

WOMAN: You care about me. A woman senses these things.

FIRST SON: What else do you sense?

WOMAN: You're playing games with me. You're lying.

FIRST SON: I wouldn't...

WOMAN: Lying is your habit, your addiction. You revel in it.

FIRST SON: You're wrong about me.

WOMAN: I wish I were. Damned child, son of a doomed mother.

FIRST SON: What do you know about me?

WOMAN: Only what I sense.

FIRST SON: You're the liar.

WOMAN: Quick boy. Quick with the lip. Up to no good, are you?

FIRST SON: Look, I just want to –

WOMAN: What?

FIRST SON: ...Aren't you going to kiss me?

WOMAN: I'm taken already. I can't have you.

FIRST SON: Husband?

WOMAN: No one else comes in between.

FIRST SON: Something sweet. Tender skin. You could hold me.

WOMAN: Is that all you want?

FIRST SON: More than anything.

WOMAN: ...What a funny boy you are standing on my beach.

FIRST SON: Don't you feel anything for me?

WOMAN: You're trespassing.

FIRST SON: This beach is yours?

WOMAN: Everybody knows that. It's private. What'd you think? Pristine sand just takes care of itself? You've got a lot to learn. Where'd you come from?

FIRST SON: The sea.

WOMAN: Water angel? Is that what you are?

FIRST SON: I don't know.

WOMAN: Lost boy.

FIRST SON: I'm not.

WOMAN: You've got blood on you.

FIRST SON: Don't...

WOMAN: I'm only...

FIRST SON: It's a stain; nothing more.

WOMAN: You should wash it off. You should be cleaned. You can't walk around like that. What will people say?

FIRST SON: They'll say what they say.

WOMAN: We're civilized here. Understand? As soon as blood comes upon us, we get rid of it. We erase everything. ...These brief days we forget, and only after do we lament. Come on now, let's get you clean. ...What is it? What are you looking at?

FIRST SON: ...Did you really see him?

WOMAN: Who?

FIRST SON: The younger ...

WOMAN: ...Funny boy. What a funny boy you are. Are you a boy?

FIRST SON: Yes.

WOMAN: You don't have to be.

She takes his hand. They go within.

3.

From outside, the Second Son spies on the First Son, who is within (the house) with the Woman. Faint music is heard from within. The Woman is showing the First Son around, engaged in the niceties of social entertaining: drinks, appetizers, a dance. The Second Son watches with fascination.

SECOND SON: I see him now.

He is inside the bosom of the house.

He is dancing close with his mannequin.

He glides. He laughs.

I reach out,

But he can't see me.

He is blind now.

He moves in another's orbit,

Touched by another's lightning.

I follow him in my own way.

I learn from what I see,

from what he teaches me.

I have only been taught to follow

Since the day I was born.

I remember. You see?

The younger boy imitates the older boy,

The second son imitates the first.

Seek none other, for he makes your path.

It has been writ down time immemorial.

In the green eye

Of the poisoned world

Hell came

And stayed for a visit.

Behold me here:

The unmade son

Awake to his demise,

And not afraid to meet it.

Drown me. Come on.

I'm willing.

For I will rise

And be sovereign one day.

The Second son looks toward the house, and then runs away.

4.

Waves. The coming night. The broadcast is heard now, a little closer.

(VO): No word still on whether the two young boys found two days ago were murdered or were victims of a ritual sacrifice, but all roads to the beach have been closed as investigation continues on the incidents surrounding this bizarre crime. There are no suspects thus far. And police are viewing the convenience store tapes for any clues that may help them piece together the facts of this sad case. Meanwhile, cross-examination has begun in the trial of the teen princess accused of strangling her lover's baby. An official statement is expected from the young woman's mother later today.

5.

Inside the house all is white and gleaming. Woman bathes the First Son: a ritual cleansing.

WOMAN: First the face: Beautiful

Expectant. Innocent. Clear, pure water. Yes.

And a hint of lemon. On the temples. And the hairline. Such a smooth fore-head. You've the perfect age, you know. There's a time in a boy's life when he is a radiant being;

Men grow to be handsome, but this... radiance... this...beauty...doesn't come back. You don't believe me?

FIRST SON: I think you're falling in love with me.

WOMAN: I'm taken, remember?

FIRST SON: So, where is he?

WOMAN: Over there. You can't see him, but he's there. He always watches me.

FIRST SON: What?

WOMAN: Don't worry. We've an arrangement.

FIRST SON: What kind?

WOMAN: Are you going to let me do this properly? Relax now.

And the torso... you're strong, aren't you?

I can feel it. Right here. Are you ticklish?

FIRST SON: No.

WOMAN: You're blushing. Just like a girl. How sweet you are. Such slim hips...

FIRST SON: Stop it.

WOMAN: What's wrong?

FIRST SON: I should leave.

WOMAN: I'm not done yet.

FIRST SON: I don't need to be bathed. I'm fine as is.

WOMAN: Come now. Don't be angry. Young boys shouldn't be marred by anger.

FIRST SON: I'm not as young as you think.

WOMAN: Indulge me, first of firsts.

FIRST SON: Why?

WOMAN: I care for you. And you need me.

FIRST SON: I don't need anybody.

WOMAN: How are you going to get by in this world? Tell me.

FIRST SON: I'm strong. I can do things.

WOMAN: Like...?

FIRST SON: I've got skills.

WOMAN: What kind?

FIRST SON: I've got a good eye for things.

WOMAN: Numbers, you mean, the economy?

FIRST SON: Yeah. Maybe. I can figure things out.

WOMAN: You don't know anything. It's nothing to be ashamed of. Ignorance is a kind of fuel, really. You can't imagine how far you can go in this world with your kind of ignorance.

FIRST SON: ...Teach me things.

WOMAN: I will.

FIRST SON: Teach me now.

WOMAN: We've plenty of time.

FIRST SON: Do we?

WOMAN: So scared, you are. Why is that? Are you frightened of me?

FIRST SON: No. I like you.

WOMAN: ... Let me anoint you.

FIRST SON: What are you doing?

WOMAN: First the limbs... hands...the tips of your fingers...

She kisses his hands.

FIRST SON: Why'd you do that?

WOMAN: To feel your skin with my lips.

FIRST SON: I don't like it. I don't want anybody kissing my hands. You understand me? I won't have it.

WOMAN: What would you have, then?

FIRST SON: Kiss on the lips, yeah. Neck, shoulders...

WOMAN: Forehead?

FIRST SON: If you like. Sure.

She kisses his forehead gently.

The Husband is seen in the background; he has a discreet view.

...You're good to me. So very good. Why is that?

WOMAN: Because I want to be. Isn't that enough?

FIRST SON: Nobody's good for long. Nobody's innocent. At the least provocation, everything can turn.

WOMAN: Is that what you remember?

FIRST SON: I remember words, yeah.

Sorrow's breath. I remember being loved once

and that love transforming itself into a monster.

WOMAN: Is that what you think I am?

FIRST SON: You could be anything. We've all got a changing shape.

WOMAN: Here. Put this on.

She offers him a necklace.

FIRST SON: It's yours.

WOMAN: It was a gift. Let it be my gift to you: An ornament for your naked beauty.

FIRST SON: I don't understand you.

WOMAN: You don't have to. Just take it.

FIRST SON: What kind of stone is -?

WOMAN: Amber.

FIRST SON: But it's violet.

WOMAN: It's a rare kind.

FIRST SON: Precious, then?

WOMAN: Very.

FIRST SON: It feels nice. (*She drapes an ankle-length garment on him.*) What are you dressing me as?

WOMAN: The noblest of men.

FIRST SON: Do men wear such things?

WOMAN: Such things and more. If you'll have me.

FIRST SON: I thought you were taken.

WOMAN: Un-take me.

FIRST SON: You want to destroy me.

WOMAN: I want what's best for you.

Don't you see? There's this woman who killed her son. They say she killed him just like that.

Without a thought. Without the slightest remorse. She had everything arranged.

The sooner the child was out of her life,

the better. They say she kissed him and stifled his breath, and watched his eyes fade from light. They say she will not be forgiven.

Would you forgive me?

FIRST SON: I don't know what you mean.

WOMAN: If I were a monster, would you forgive me? Would you protect me?

FIRST SON: Is this what you do: steal boys from your beach? Steal them away and make of them meat?

WOMAN: Oh, sweet boy, act the dutiful daughter, and not the vengeful son. Do not let fear be your guide as you wake now to this new world. There's no need to be afraid, my dear boy, for you are learning to speak the language of the dead.

She kisses him on the mouth, overtaking him. Husband disappears from view.

6.

The Second Son is at road's edge. He is met by Nurse, a man in well-worn beach clothes: capri pants, a colorful shirt, and sandals.

NURSE: I think she pushed those boys in. Yeah. Right into the water. Left them to drown like that, all gussied up like girls.

I'm sure it was her, this woman I saw.

I'm sure she did it. She's got the look of a murderer. A real elegant type. She was driving a car. Fancy. Latest model. I can't afford that. I haven't the money, know what I mean? I'm not in her class. But she... oh yeah. She had jewels on. Emeralds and amber...I saw her. Not at the convenience store, but after...I don't know why nobody will interview me. I'm a witness, right? I could tell things and make a fortune.

But nobody will ask me. They just say those boys are dead and that's that. And it means nothing to nobody cause boys die all the time:

In woods, ravines, trenches, mines...Some boys are dead even when they're alive; They come home from wars and lock-ups And they're dead inside. Know what I mean? ...You're a boy, aren't you? You're a pretty little thing waiting to be screwed.

You've got fresh face, and small hands. Long limbs. ...I could go up right inside you. Would you like that? Damned boy. Don't you speak?

SECOND SON: I don't need words.

NURSE: How much, then?

SECOND SON: What you'll give me?

NURSE: Is this what you know?

SECOND SON: Pure love doesn't exist. I know that. There was a young boy who told an older boy to take care of him, but the older boy turned the other way, and only took care of himself. What was the younger boy to do

but turn himself away, away to another world, too? What use have I for sweet words, or for love?

NURSE: You talk like you're in disguise.

SECOND SON: Do you mind?

NURSE: You can use another's tongue but you best learn it right. Best not slip.

SECOND SON: I'll take your advice.

NURSE: I wouldn't take it to heart. I'm a failure at life. Anxious hands, anxious deeds, a bit of screwing and some crystal does me.

Do you want to go for a ride?

SECOND SON: Where to?

NURSE: Spin round the city. See the sky.

I got a portable wonderland, right?

SECOND SON: You'll protect me?

NURSE: I don't get boys like you into trouble. It's not in my nature.

SECOND SON: Swear?

NURSE: I promise.

SECOND SON: ...All right.

NURSE: ...You're an easy type. We're going to get on just fine. What is it? You're cold?

SECOND SON: A little.

NURSE: Need some good hands to do you a survey? "Survey the merchandise. Make sure that it's clean." That's what my mom always said. My mom was an angel. Was yours an angel, pigeon?

SECOND SON: I don't remember.

NURSE: Orphan boy. Is that what you are? An orphaned thing spit out from mother ocean?

SECOND SON: Sent back to shore, I think.

NURSE: A prince, a right sovereign.

How far must you have come, my pigeon...

How very far to find yourself here in this tatty world. Got yourself a name?

SECOND SON: No.

NURSE: ..."I have no name

I am but two days old. –

What shall I call thee?

I happy am.

Joy is my name, -

Sweet joy befall thee!

Pretty joy!

Sweet joy but two days old.

Sweet joy I call thee."[1]

SECOND SON: Joy. Yes. Joy is my name.

NURSE: Wet kiss, then?

SECOND SON: I've not much practice.

NURSE: You're slipping, pigeon.

Keep your disguise, dear Joy, sweet Joy of mine. Listen to your nurse. She knows you from the womb, from your day of making.

SECOND SON: How much did you see, sweet Nurse?

NURSE: You mean of the elegant lady and the like? Of the real live story?

SECOND SON: Yes.

NURSE: I saw everything, my little one, that I did. Come now, be released, dear Joy. Be released through me.

And the Nurse leads Second Son away.

---

1 William Blake, "Infant Joy."

7.

Night. The First son walks proudly through the silvery house while Woman and her Husband make love.

FIRST SON: I walk

through the house of familiar objects

Wearing the clothes of a beauteous daughter.

I smell of honey, and myrtle

And cling to the amber that adorns me.

This is my home now, I tell myself.

This is how I shall live in this new world

That has taken me in

And has saved me

from wandering the curved earth

In search of a false memory.

I hear the woman and her husband make love in the barren room.

And I remember the smell of sex,

And how a younger boy kissed me

because he knew no one else

And how I returned his kiss

with pride and diffidence.

Words, you see. They come back to me.

I am piecing together who I can be

From this I hear, and this I see:

The passionate scream, and the silver tray resting on the stone centerpiece,

The guttural moan, and the golden rings woven into the obscene tapestry.

I remember everything and nothing,

As I continue walking

Through the resplendent house

Of empty rooms surrounded by the sea.

Look at me, I cry.

Look at me, I sing.

I am your guardian; I am your mercenary.

Stir my limbs and fill me with vengeance

Even as I act the daughter dear,

The delicate thing,

Made for your sport

and your errant amusement.

Hold me up on a sublime pedestal.

Venus' envy am I.

And then I remember the younger boy

Who sought his comfort in my anxiety.

He was familiar to me, too.

A twinned self, a blood thing

Lost in the waves, drowned by my inconstancy.

Poor boy, I whisper

To no one.

How I miss your unpracticed tongue,

Your tender lips,

And open heart.

Poor lost boy,

What has become of you here

in this new world

Which prizes nothing

except the warmth of flesh

Against the cold massacre of night?

8.

Sex spent, and wanting more, the Second Son is fed by the Nurse, and then readied for trade.

NURSE: You're a ravenous one.

SECOND SON: I crave...

NURSE: Too much. Suck at my tit, and left me empty, you have.

SECOND SON: Been long time since...

NURSE: No need to say it. Here. Here's a bit of sugar. That'll keep you for a while. Don't ever say you don't know nothing. Not to anybody else, y'hear? Cause it won't get you anywhere, Joy, and you want to go places, don't you?

You want to see things?

SECOND SON: Whole world. Yes. That's what I want. Never seen anything except what's before me. Tall woman once – like you – you remind me of her, you do – She held me for days and then no more. It was like I'd been sent to a dark place. A place of full of tears that knows no end, because weeping doesn't stop,

And history isn't over, even if we think it is. Isn't that right, Nurse?

NURSE: You're getting ideas in your head. I don't know what to make of it.

SECOND SON: Make of it what you will. Trade me for what I'm worth, which is plenty, and you know it.

NURSE: Worth a bundle, if you keep your sweetness intact. Ripe boy, you are. That's true enough.

SECOND SON: I'm ripe for the taking, even after I've been took.

NURSE: Sweet Joy, you're made a man.

SECOND SON: Through and through.

NURSE: And yet worth more as a girl,

As a changeable thing for precious Joy is what we seek come night fall, come daybreak.

Precious dear and awfully willing. Men get shot, boys get killed, and it's the girl ones, who keep going. Remember that. For after I'm gone,

you will need to know these things so as not to swim in the dark ocean full of tears like a lost babe caught in the current ready to be swept out to Hades. Promise me you'll remember.

SECOND SON: I do.

NURSE: There, there. Such vacant eyes need rest. Sugar's sleep is what you need.

SECOND SON: Tit in mouth is what I want. Suckle me, sweet Nurse. Send me back to the womb.

NURSE: Fist, Joy. Hard fist now. No more suckling. Done enough for to-night.

I know you want and want, but I'm empty, y'hear? I get sick fast, see? That's my calamity.

Best you go on now; put on clothes that suit your trade. Pick something there. I've got fresh market goods.

SECOND SON: Jeans and halters?

NURSE: No. Not for you, Joy.

You need some sheer lace to show off your torso, the cut of your figure must be appreciated by all. There. That's a smile. You like compliments, eh?

SECOND SON: I like being told nice things.

NURSE: Don't get too accustomed to it, dear. Compliments spoil us. Rough words sometimes do better than kind. Those tap pants are nice. Silk, eh?

SECOND SON: You mind?

And the Second Son starts to put on the lingerie,

the old clothes for his new life...

NURSE: No. You need vintage style

to remind us all of the past,

Of the good rolling times

Of quick money, and

And all manner of ripe pickings

just waiting round the corner

Singing sweet jazz,

Coming foul in the mouth,

And letting all the workers down low

Rise up to the high life,

To riches and glory, right?

Do you know what I'm talking about, pigeon?

Do you what I mean by jazz?

I'm teaching you things, Joy.

I'm teaching you how to get by in this life.

SECOND SON: *[dressed now]* I'm grateful, sweet Nurse.

NURSE: As well you should be, pigeon.

I've no riches except what comes from a lifetime of work and caring, and of being a good nurse to all those in need, you see?

SECOND SON: One day I'll be...

NURSE: No. Not you. Not a nurse.

You're a prince, dear. You've got shining future ahead of you. I can see this. I have visions. Just like I'd seen that lady in the car

and those boys...I see things. You're to go far, pigeon.

SECOND SON: I've visions, too. I've seen things.

NURSE: Past hauntings?

SECOND SON: Future ones, I think.

NURSE: What do you see, child?

SECOND SON: A divine image:

A boy stands veiled in blood,

unsure of himself, unsure of everything.

He trembles. He waits.

A shiver song caught in his throat.

A tall woman appears.

She looks at him with soft eyes. She holds him.

And sings him to sleep.

Nurse pulls Second Son toward him, and sings:

"Orphan Boy"

Poor orphan boy.

Come right out of water

Seeking where to dream.

Come right out of water

Looking for where he'd been.

Orphan, orphan boy

Rest your pretty head.

No reason to this world.

No reason once you're dead.

Lights dim on Nurse and Second Son. In the house, Woman and First Son are
illuminated. The First Son looks at himself in a mirror. He wears a new garment.

FIRST SON: How you love me...

WOMAN: Yes.

FIRST SON: Because I'm the most beautiful?

WOMAN: Perhaps.

FIRST SON: You know it's true.

WOMAN: You are exquisite.

FIRST SON: I am ravishing.

WOMAN: Careful now.

FIRST SON: What'd you mean?

WOMAN: You must not yield to your beauty.

FIRST SON: Why not?

WOMAN: Remember: it will be short-lived.

FIRST SON: What of it? It's what we make of things that count.

WOMAN: In the here and now?

FIRST SON: Yes.

WOMAN: Cursed boy.

FIRST SON: Ravishing boy.

WOMAN: ...Don't lose yourself, dear.

FIRST SON: What'd you mean?

WOMAN: Let me keep you here. This is sanctuary.

FIRST SON: Admire me, then. Worship me. For I am what you make of me.

WOMAN: Greedy boy. ...What am I going to do with you?

FIRST SON: Take care of me. Sing to me.

Woman sings another section of "Orphan Boy" song,

while the First Son revels.

WOMAN: The weight of water,

Oh tender child,

leaves ancient sorrow

far behind.

The still of sundown

on borrowed time

will ease your trouble

...clear your mind.

Fade up on Nurse and Second son. Nurse sings.

NURSE: Orphan, orphan boy

Dream a thing or two,

For there will be another

who dreams a dream of you.

Nurse cradles the Second son. First Son stands in adoration before the Woman who caresses him. Lights fade.

9.

Waves. The broadcast is heard, a little closer still.

(VO): Police continue to investigate the alleged murder of the two boys found on the beach the other day. No mention has been made yet of the boys' names or where they were from. Media attention focuses instead on the trial of the teen princess, who will take the stand in her defense tomorrow morning. Sources say that the young woman has been distraught the last few days, and worried about her appearance. Check your local stations for up-to-the-minute news on this and other breaking stories. Weather in the 90s, winds to the north, and rain expected later in the week.

10.

It is near daybreak. Inside the house, the First Son is seen through the glass.

FIRST SON: I sleep, and pretend

I am you and he at one and the same.

I slip off my daughter's clothes

– my clean things –

And imitate your sounds.

My mouth opens. Fire breathes...

Never leave, I wish. Never leave, I cry.

Stare at my eyelids. Watch me.

I am your remnant of memory.

Reach out your hand, open my senses.

Lead me. You do everything out of love.

The glass turns and Husband and Woman are seen, entwined.

HUSBAND: He moves.

WOMAN: He waits for us.

HUSBAND: He listens.

WOMAN: He won't stop until he's had his fill.

HUSBAND: He's addicted.

WOMAN: Yes.

HUSBAND: To our sex.

WOMAN: To our needs.

HUSBAND: What shall we do?

WOMAN: Love him. What else can we do?

HUSBAND: ...Before there was no one.

WOMAN: And now there is another, here, with us.

HUSBAND: Between us.

WOMAN: Joining us.

HUSBAND: Closer.

WOMAN: And even closer.

HUSBAND: ...He needs us.

WOMAN: He has no one.

HUSBAND: Poor boy.

WOMAN: He sings.

HUSBAND: Very softly. What is it?

WOMAN: A song without words. A song of yearning for two bodies, not one....

HUSBAND: Let's show him.

WOMAN: Let's teach him everything. Such a good daughter... Such a good son.....Is he gone?

HUSBAND: He's still.

WOMAN: He's transfixed. Tender child...

HUSBAND: He watches you like one. Full of love. Pure love. I can't look at him anymore. His eyes burn into me. You've brought this boy here to vex my heart.

WOMAN: I've done nothing of the kind. Know this: I love you now more than before. His presence stirs me... The thread which crosses through him to you is destined for me, for he is like you: made for me. And I am the path from thread to line, from line to thread and back.

I am complete.

HUSBAND: What words are these?

WOMAN: A lover's words.

HUSBAND: A mother's words.

WOMAN: If unconditional love is what you seek...? Then yes, perhaps yes, a mother's words.

HUSBAND: And for me, for your lover, what words are there left?

WOMAN: The same words only red, violet and orange in hue.

HUSBAND: I dream in red, the color of blood, yes but I also dream of regret and of waking to not find you.

WOMAN: But I'm here, right here... What is it? Tell me.

HUSBAND: The boy's staring.

WOMAN: You imagine him.

HUSBAND: No. He's here. Right here, behind the glass.

WOMAN: He's on the sand; he's strolling the beach, stretching his legs... He's finding himself slowly. Let him be.

HUSBAND: He's in my eyes. His sweetness is consuming. Hungry boy...

WOMAN: Call to him, then.

HUSBAND: What for?

WOMAN: Let's ravage him. Split him.

HUSBAND: Gut him.

WOMAN: Lover dear, husband dear...

HUSBAND: Claw...

WOMAN: Bite. Scratch.

HUSBAND: Woo me anew.

WOMAN: With spite.

HUSBAND: I fell in love with you through and through. From first I saw. That was clear.

You were my cup of sweet poison, my rich jewel ready to be worn.

WOMAN: And haven't I given you everything, husband dear?

HUSBAND: Too much... your bitter taste cuts through me...

WOMAN: Lustful boy.

HUSBAND: Man, not boy. A boy is he who stands there like a little girl waiting for us to part.

WOMAN: Loose yourself... Abandon yourself to me. Consume me in your fire, make of me ash, for out of it we shall both rise.

HUSBAND: In triumph, dear, exceeding...

Husband and Woman make love.

11.

Morning. The house is serene. Woman and the First Son are eating. Silence.

FIRST SON: The harlot of the blood knot.

WOMAN: Those are cheery words. Did you sleep all right?

FIRST SON: I didn't sleep at all. I couldn't sleep, could I? You were with him.

WOMAN: He is my husband. I told you when we met that I was taken. I've never lied to you. Do you want me to start now?

FIRST SON: No.

WOMAN: Then don't sulk. Please. It's not becoming. Keep your face up.

FIRST SON: Yes, dear.

WOMAN: You're brooding. It's to be expected, I suppose.

FIRST SON: Why? Cause I'm a boy?

WOMAN: You're still learning the ways of the world.

FIRST SON: Crap world this. Rotten, aching… blisters on the sand.

WOMAN: Drink your tea.

FIRST SON: Are you going to play "the mother" now?

WOMAN: I don't play roles. I'm not an actor.

FIRST SON: And yet you change. From one moment to the next…

WOMAN: So do we all. Terror, cruelty, and jealousy all have a human face.

FIRST SON: What am I? Eh? What am I to you?

WOMAN: You're beautiful. That's enough. You're my angel, my sacred apparition, my first of firsts.

FIRST SON: …Silly harlot.

WOMAN: Watch your tongue.

FIRST SON: Why should I?

WOMAN: Because this is my house.

FIRST SON: His house, where he beds you.

WOMAN: And goes inside me, yes. Don't forget. You're well-kept, and fed, and you're safe here. What more do you want, dear boy?

FIRST SON: More than more. I want everything.

WOMAN: (tenderly) Have a pear.

FIRST SON: I'm not hungry.

WOMAN: You need to fill yourself.

FIRST SON: With what? Poison? I have that already. Have plenty. It's all inside me.

I can feel it. My blood's swimming poison.

WOMAN: Do you think I am giving my affection to a third party when it should rightfully be given to you?

FIRST SON: What's that? Babble-talk?

WOMAN: It's a question, that's all. I claimed you, but you do not claim me. My affection is free. My attention and love are granted as I please.

FIRST SON: And what do I get?

WOMAN: The best tea, this house, the beach...

the perfect attainment of your beauty, such as it is, for it will be short-lived. ...How I do grieve for you...

FIRST SON: Already?

WOMAN: I grieve eternally. My suffering knows no bounds. Can't you see?

FIRST SON: I see someone who seizes ruin,

Whose heart gives way to secrecy. Idle hope you should have that I will ever nurse you in your old age and deck your corpse with loving hands. I'll do no such thing. I'm not made for it. I'll not repay you in kind for any mercy granted me. You will lose me in time; I'll see to it. And I'll never again look at you with fond eyes. Bitterness and sorrow will be your company at your life's end. That's what I see in my tabloid memory.

WOMAN: Pity me, my dear boy; see me through and through, as I see you.

We are both wronged in ecstasy.

We both crave, and seal our fate

With too much love, so much ardor,

zealous we are in our *jalousie.*

For in love, this love,

In its faint ray we regard

Anger

Blame,

Doubt,

Ignorance

Virtue

Safety

And privacy

While we entertain

Abuse

Duty

Panic

Despair

Freedom

And pollution.

Our presence, my presence and yours too,

is a pollution

And yet we make of it something holy, yes.

A pollution of saints

Bound by love.

You see, sweet boy? Strange boy...

My son and daughter at once,

So much have you to learn,

And so much you have learned already

At my hands

By my bed

Through my dignity.

Steal your heart now;

you will be the better for it.

FIRST SON: ...It's early.

WOMAN: So it is.

FIRST SON: Day's just begun.

WOMAN: And what's in store for us?

FIRST SON: Whatever you wish.

12.

Husband behind the glass.

HUSBAND: Woo him with my words.

Take him into your heart.

Clever glittering creature,

Wrap him tight

And dispose of me.

You are a changing being.

This is what I see:

You let the boy in.

You toy with him as if he were your son,

"Our son,

The first of firsts,"

and you watch him move

like an errant daughter.

You wrap him inside your tongue

Which has a serpent's will.

And he follows

Unknowing

Blissful

As if in a dream.

Sweet boy he is...your boy...not mine...

for he is meant for me, and not for me.

Fear disintegrates my throat,

and you eat happily,

as I contemplate a barren feast.

What is he to you

But a little nothing?

How can a woman love so completely

and without shame?

I see you true, my passionate beast.

You who were my soul's fire

have turned into a bauble,

a mock lover,

bent on deceiving me.

Mutilated hours

mark my days.

Cold evenings

Wreck my heart.

Our sex is but a feverish lightning.

Damp sheets, crushed pillows

And the imprint of your body.

We live on a broken ship,

Mastless

And bereft of sails.

13.

On the boardwalk where the boys cruise as girl-boys at morning's rise, the
Second Son wears his new life clothes. The Nurse is his guide.

Note: This is played in the spirit of a vaudeville turn.

SECOND SON: I'd like to contribute to the future discourse

NURSE: on mourning

SECOND SON: I can tell you a thing or two

about negotiating with the dead

NURSE: and living at times in the Underworld.

SECOND SON: I've been fetched, you see,

by demons and daemons.

My history is not revealed easily.

NURSE: Some say history is over

but I don't believe them.

I think all you have to do is look at the fine print

SECOND SON: all around

NURSE: and it's clear

SECOND SON: that history is alive,

NURSE: and doing its repetitive dance

SECOND SON: of death, mayhem, joy,

NURSE: and good old-fashioned ecstasy.

Take our siren, our dame of note:

she has her hooks in,

her locks in place

and she's ready to roll.

What care anyone for a little blood spilt?

We must all have our sacrifice,

our sweet honey jazz.

Look here,

SECOND SON: Look here,

See what we're made of – you and I:

NURSE: the same stuff

NURSE & SECOND SON: Altogether

SECOND SON: That's right

NURSE: And if you think different

SECOND SON: woe to you

NURSE: Sweet honey woe

What destiny awaits you

if you think you're above the melee.

SECOND SON: Hey Babycakes

come over here, and put your flesh on the line.

It's time to serve your country,

to be dutiful and proud

and not look back

at what history can teach you,

at what surely awaits us all

if we pay attention to what's gone before,

past, over and out.

Hey Sugar

press your lips

for the grand economy of style.

NURSE: for petrol, tobacco, rum, cold sex, and sweet cane the world over
SECOND SON: *[To Nurse]*

(given up by Cain the brother in ancient time;

but that was old blood, right? We'll have none of it now)

[back to the clientele]

I wave my hand, Babycakes

secure in the knowledge

that no one will know that tomorrow

NURSE: in Pakistan,

or in the new China,

which has superseded Barcelona *und* Berlin,

as the It spot of it spots where one needs to be seen,

SECOND SON: a boy will be found strangled by his own economic dreams.

NURSE: This is the way of the sorry-ass world

SECOND SON: This is what we crave:

NURSE: blood and death

SECOND SON: blood and sex

blood

NURSE: and more blood...

on an immaculate tray.

And the Second Son strikes a burlesque pose on a makeshift pedestal.

14.

On the boardwalk Husband sees the Second Son in his new guise, and takes him aside

Out of slight view

For an exchange

Of anonymous sex

And no talk.

Just passionate fury

And extreme release

15.

Woman sees Husband and the Second Son make love in her mind's eye

WOMAN: Doubt enters. It fills me up.

It burrows deep. My heart is torn by doubt.

I can't touch him now

without thinking he's with someone else.

I am ravaged by thoughts and whispers.

I punish myself.

But punishment serves no purpose when doubt remains.

Doubt is a poison. It infects the blood. And once it is in your veins,

there is little you can do but give in to it slowly, and let everything fade.

I say goodbye to him each morning.

I kiss his empty pillow and become accustomed to his absence.

I am learning how to live without love.

This lesson I am teaching myself,

so I can go on.

Each day I doubt him more.

One day I will lose him completely.

I am consumed.

My vision is corrupted. I breathe doubt.

I taste it. I hold it on my tongue.

I ask nothing and imagine everything.'

While in mirrored frames

The First Son sees Husband and Woman make love in his mind's eye.

Husband sees Woman and First Son make love in his mind's eye.

The Second Son sees First Son in clear-eyed memory,

as the Nurse sings reprise of "Orphan Boy"

NURSE: Orphan, orphan boy

Dream a thing or two

for there will be another

who dreams a dream of you.

16.

The gleaming house readies for slaughter.

Woman is waiting. Husband walks in.

WOMAN: Late.

HUSBAND: What?

WOMAN: You're late.

HUSBAND: You've never minded before.

WOMAN: I'm here in this house. I wait. I watch the sea turn black. I watch the sand curl up, and the gulls pick at the ground with their hideous beaks.

HUSBAND: What's this? A soliloquy?

WOMAN: I saw you.

HUSBAND: What are you talking about?

WOMAN: With her.

HUSBAND: I don't know who you mean.

WOMAN: Your whore.

HUSBAND: Are you following me?

WOMAN: I don't need to. You're out in the open. The whole world can see.

HUSBAND: ...Does it disgust you?

WOMAN: My passion and my beauty are not sufficient for your needs?

HUSBAND: The veneer of artifice and civilization repels me. You see, love without betrayal doesn't mean anything. Without cruelty, there is no feast. We all do what we need.

WOMAN: Really? And what is that?

HUSBAND: You've the boy, don't you?

WOMAN: My boy... he's a figment, a sweet thing, an innocent being. That's all. An apparition.

HUSBAND: A flesh and blood apparition.

WOMAN: Are you out of love with me?

HUSBAND: ...Get some sleep.

WOMAN: Pacify her. Tranquilize her. Sedate her. Isn't that what you mean?

HUSBAND: We forge what we want out of what we have. I don't complain.

WOMAN: My passion is twice yours.

HUSBAND: You believe what you need to believe.

WOMAN: Don't silence me.

HUSBAND: I'm doing nothing of the kind.

WOMAN: You ignore me. You shut me out. Come to bed with me. Or would you rather have me cold-assed on the boardwalk like your good whore?

HUSBAND: A whore fuck is the purest fuck.

WOMAN: ...Was she alive, then, your whore?

HUSBAND: Alive and warm as far as I could tell.

WOMAN: Was he?

Pause.

HUSBAND: How much did you see?

WOMAN: Answer me.

HUSBAND: He had flesh like a girl, if that's what you mean. Just like your boy. A somewhat transient thing. I gave, he received. He didn't really want me, but the rules were clear. There was no talk. Love's delusion didn't get in the way, and that made me love him all the more. In the manner in which I prefer.

WOMAN: Anonymously?

HUSBAND: The most personal act of intimacy engaged through the most impersonal circumstance. Yes. That is truth. The rest is lies.

WOMAN: Our lie?

HUSBAND: Yes. Yes. The lie of convenience: marriage, a fine house, money, social standing, power, privacy, at the expense of lust, sensation, and knowledge.

WOMAN: If you love me still, then love me as you would, and I'll return your harshness in kind.

HUSBAND: Shall I nail you, then? Shall I take you from behind? Which position would you like? Shall I crucify you like the unholy saint that you pretend to be? Would you like that, dear wife?

WOMAN: I'd like nothing more.

HUSBAND: What game is this?

WOMAN: A game of fury.

HUSBAND: Hell's fury...

WOMAN: Vengeance in my mouth.

HUSBAND: Trembling tongue, though.

WOMAN: This is the game of living, of life itself. The mischief is just beginning.

HUSBAND: Dirty...

WOMAN: Sublime,

HUSBAND: Decaying

WOMAN: Beautiful

HUSBAND: Extreme.

WOMAN: I know no bounds, love. Know this about me.

HUSBAND: ...Until the boy...

WOMAN: Save your blame for another.

HUSBAND: We live in the darkest poverty of desire. And yet you want more.

WOMAN: Undo me. Yes.

HUSBAND: Harsh want.

WOMAN: A test of your true self.

HUSBAND: Very well then. This is as pure and honest as I'll ever be. Take off your clothes, strip away your finery. If this is a life-game, then let's play it. Let's exploit each other. I'm not taking anything, and you're not giving anything. The only barter here is flesh.

First Son appears.

FIRST SON: Don't touch her.

WOMAN: Get away from here, child. You've none of me. Not now.

FIRST SON: I've all of you. You promised me.

WOMAN: I didn't promise anything.

FIRST SON: What do you mean?

WOMAN: I never said...

FIRST SON: You wanted me from the first. You watched me sleep. I remember. "Soft eyelids," you said.

WOMAN: Dear, sweet boy...

FIRST SON: Stop treating me like a child!

HUSBAND: ...Which one will you choose, dear? The tender skin, the tired kisses,

the unconditional cuddle as would a likely son to a likely mother? Or this mirror, your true mirror, which will never be in danger of ever becoming mired in beauty?

WOMAN: ...Get out.

FIRST SON: This is my house, too. You said you'd keep me.

HUSBAND: As a kept girl. Am I right? As a little plaything.

FIRST SON: Shut up.

HUSBAND: Boys will be boys.

WOMAN: I can't keep you, dear. Don't you see? If you know what's best for you, if you care anything for me, walk away now.

There's time.

FIRST SON: What words are those? You learnt them from some book or something?

HUSBAND: They're words. As good as any.

FIRST SON: You've nothing to say to me.

HUSBAND: I don't know you.

FIRST SON: Love ceases, eh? Just like that?

WOMAN: I cut love out. Yes.

FIRST SON: You lie.

WOMAN: I always have.

FIRST SON: False woman?

HUSBAND: Falser than you think. I know her better than you. I've got the full view, son.

Do as she says. Walk away. Take a stroll. Feel the sand under your feet; feel its warmth; it will heal you.

FIRST SON: Go swimming?

HUSBAND: Yes. It's a good sport. Clears the mind.

FIRST SON: ...Something tender, sweet...

WOMAN: Don't.

FIRST SON: Hold me. Please.

WOMAN: ...Go.

FIRST SON: ...Liar.

WOMAN: Believe what you need...

FIRST SON: I don't need anything.

First Son takes off the amber necklace, tossing it at her feet, and leaves.

HUSBAND: The boy gone. Silence falls. No whispers here now. No figures behind the glass. It's just us.

WOMAN: What's left of us.

HUSBAND: Get used to it, dear. If you want to see me again. What I do is what I do.

He takes off his belt.

Wherever, whomever I seek...

He stands behind her, and places belt at her throat.

WOMAN: Get off me.

HUSBAND: It's what you want, how you want... pure extreme.

He takes her from behind by force.

Close-up on the Woman's face, transfigured.

17.

Waves. The broadcast can be barely heard midst static.

(VO): Today...

in the murder...

the teen princess...

Said to be...

live...

"And I just want to say that in my heart..."

This is live...

Cruelty...

In other...

Times.

Static.

First Son stands at road's edge ready for trade, and is met by the Nurse.

NURSE: We are all disgraceful, obscene, and debased here. That's the truth of our beings.

No sense looking up in this world. It's just sky. Nothing else up there. No saints looking down on us, judging our deeds.

Look down, stay close to the ground.

Sex breaks the rational mind. You follow me?

FIRST SON: Maybe. Yeah.

NURSE: You're smart. I can see that. You've got some sense. Just waylaid, am I right?

Lost your place?

FIRST SON: Yes.

NURSE: "The little boy lost in the lonely fen,

Led by the wandering light..."[2]

FIRST SON: Thrown out, yeah. She'll have none of me.

NURSE: It's a pity. Fine boy like you.

Oh, I just look, that's all. I'm no one in this world. I keep low, safe. Nothing hurts me.... Heard the story?

FIRST SON: What?

NURSE: Over the waves.

FIRST SON: No.

NURSE: Got acquitted, she did.

FIRST SON: Who?

NURSE: A teen princess. Acquitted of murder. She killed her kid. Choked him in revenge. Her man was cheating on her. Turns out it was for love, not vengeance, that she did it. Said "Oh, I'm sorry," like an apology is enough. Like simple words are going to wipe the soul clean. Strange what people do, say... I think she should've gotten the highest penalty.

FIRST SON: Hanging?

---

2   William Blake, "Little Boy Found"

NURSE: Need a hanging every once in a while to clear the air, get things moving again.

First son starts to walk away.

Like you, right? Moving about.

FIRST SON: It's all screwy.

NURSE: What is?

FIRST SON: What I'm feeling.

NURSE: Inside?

FIRST SON: I want to go back to her. She was like my tether line. She brought things back to me, you see? Things in my memory that I'd kept hidden away: affection, kisses, peaceful things....Hurt, too, but hurt's all right.

I can take it. I'm strong, yeah.

Soil and garbage are nothing to me.

I breathe them in, cause they tell me what reality is. And I'm grateful.

NURSE: You're on the meat line now.

FIRST SON: And what of it? End all, I say. Finish me. That's what I'd like. Be ended of this world. Cast me out, feed me to the ocean. Love's gone from me.

NURSE: Crapped on. Haven't we been?

FIRST SON: Yes.

NURSE: Doomed from the start. That's us. Expecting goodness, getting none,

And getting by somehow...

Cut love out, I say. Cut one, get another.

We're all expendable here in this place.

We all stand on the sand and piss on it.

FIRST SON: Yeah.

NURSE: And what we do, eh?

FIRST SON: I don't know.

NURSE: Make do, right? Like this pigeon I got. He's seen to the wise. He's got himself doing steady now.

FIRST SON: What'd you mean?

NURSE: On the boardwalk. Over there.

FIRST SON: I don't see anybody.

NURSE: Of course you do. Just look. Good look, son.

FIRST SON: The young one?

NURSE: Yeah. Joy's the name. Infant joy of mine.

FIRST SON: He's familiar somehow.

NURSE: Get a closer look, then.

FIRST SON: He's like the younger...

NURSE: Joy's young. I grant you that.

A ripe one.

FIRST SON: He kissed me on the mouth.

NURSE: Know him already?

FIRST SON: His was a pure kiss.

NURSE: The best kind, eh?

FIRST SON: I thought I'd never see him again.

NURSE: Those that are familiar should be together.

FIRST SON: ...Will he remember me?

NURSE: Infant Joy will know you. We all know our way back to love from ignorance.

You recognize him, don't you?

FIRST SON: I remember him. Yes.

NURSE: That's good enough.

FIRST SON: ...Can I get you something?

NURSE: From the store? You're a sweet thing.

FIRST SON: I'm not cheap.

NURSE: For my time and trouble, anything will do. I'm easy.... Just see to the younger.

FIRST SON: I will....What it'll be, then? Soda pop?

NURSE: Yeah...Cherry-lime.

First Son walks away.

18.

On the boardwalk, the Second Son offers himself;

He waits for nothing and everything.

SECOND SON: This is how I'm seen

As a sacrificial body

Ready to be taken

Waiting to be torn.

I let them see me like this

Cause this is what they want.

This is what they need.

I'm not a pure thing to them.

I'm an offering of love,

Which needs to be destroyed.

Right now.

Come on.

Do me in.

That's right.

That's what you're paying for, sweet:

The dead boy on your lap,

The dead boy on your altar.

This is the dead boy, live and complete

For your eternal pleasure,

And redemption.

Suffer through me,

Release yourself.

Count on the hope of this impossible exchange on the street,

To raise your position in society one hundred percent.

And once I am dead to you

I am worth ever so much more.

My market value sky-rockets

Each time I am bent

Each time I am fucked

Each time I am...

Whatever you make me.

I am your son/daughter,

father/mother

the before he, the girl she

The young thing

Waiting to be formed.

Get a look at my slim hips,

My long legs,

My fragile quivering lips

Aching for a kiss,

A real kiss

Uh-huh

Some sweet jazz, yeah.

I'll go mad if you don't come.

I'm mad already. Can't you see?

The First Son in the convenience store camera's eye with bottle of cherry-lime
soda in hand....

FIRST SON: This is the new me,

The brother sweet, the other son.

Hold me.

Don't waste any time.

This is precious.

This is how it's meant to be.

Romanticism is the world,

And I'm its empress.

SECOND SON: Box me.

Tear my flesh,

Flesh the boy now...

Place my meat on your altar.

FIRST SON: And I'll smile.

I won't feel a thing.

There's nothing to feel when you've been left.

There's only every reason to be happy.

What are you afraid of, son?

SECOND SON: What are you waiting for?

FIRST SON: When will you come back for me, mother?

SECOND SON: I'm here. Take me.

Woman approaches. After a few gestures, and an exchange of hard smiles, Woman touches the Second Son tenderly. She kisses his hands. He responds with an embrace. A moment.

She leads Second Son away toward the beach. She picks up a conch shell. She strikes the Second Son with it. A blow to the head. The Second Son falls. Time shift.

The convenience store camera watches the Woman as she motions to the First Son.

After a few moments of hesitation, She kisses him. He embraces her. A moment.

She walks away, he follows her.

They head toward the sea. The Second Son is lying on the shoreline. He is still.
The First Son goes to the Second Son. He kneels over the body of the Second Son,
which remains still. The Woman strikes the First Son with the conch shell. A blow
to the head. The First Son falls upon the Second Son's body. Their bodies are
entwined.

The Woman watches the two boys for a long time. Waves.

19.

The gleaming house is quiet. Woman stares at the sea.

Husband stands, near her.

WOMAN: I held them in my arms

your lover, my lover, our boys.

They were like children again somehow

So willing

So sweet

All anger gone

Each one indebted to my touch,

Wanting so very much

To belong to this world.

And I made them believe it.

I said Yes, come with me. You are here now. Safe.

I will protect you from all harm.

My tears will purify you.

They would believe anything,

Innocent boys,

Reckless in their ignorance.

They took our love so tenderly.

They were our amusement.

We made of them what we wanted,

Dear lovers, hard lovers,

So very dear.

How will you remember them?

As a girl? Boy?

Pliant daughter, bitter son?

Figureless figures of vanishing origin.

How will they remember us

When they wake to their demise?

What memory will be left them

In their cruel abandonment?

What will follow this perfect sacrifice?

"Of one alone, one woman alone

sent mad by heaven.

O women's love,

So full of trouble,"

They will say.

And we'll honor them,

The nattering mouths,

The gawkers and gossip-mongers.

We'll give them something to look at,

won't we?

We will be reborn.

We will escape death.

And we'll stay here in this clean, corrupt house

With only our fury to sustain us.

The whites of our eyes will be red,

Our tongues will breathe fire,

And our irises will burn.

And we'll return to our bed

Depleted of desire

yet locked by our flesh

Which will not remember

A before or after

Only now, now, eternal.

Feeble lust governed us both

And it governs us still.

There is no guard but love itself,

Innocent of knowledge.

We have claimed our hateful hearts.

No forgiveness now.

Pause. The Woman looks at her Husband. His head is down. She gestures toward the door, and they slowly walk further into the house.

CPSIA information can be obtained
at www.ICGtesting.com
Printed in the USA
LVHW112249010920
664806LV00003B/962

About the Author

Caridad Svich is a playwright-songwriter-translator and editor of Cuban-Spanish-Argentine-Croatian descent. She is the recipient of a 2012 OBIE for Lifetime Achievement in the theatre, and a 2011 Primus Prize from the American Theatre Critics Association. Among her other key works include *12 Ophelias*, *Alchemy of Desire/Dead-Man's Blues*, *Fugitive Pieces*, *The Booth Variations*, *Iphigenia...(a rave fable)*, *Instructions for Breathing*, *GUAPA*, *The Way of Water* and *The House of the Spirits* (based on the Isabel Allende novel). She has translated nearly all of Federico Garcia Lorca's plays and works by Calderon de la Barca, Lope de Vega, Julio Cortazar, Antonio Buero Vallejo and contemporary works by dramatists from Mexico , Cuba and Catalonia. She is editor of several books on theatre & performance published by Manchester University Press/UK, TCG, Eyecorner Press and Smith & Kraus. She is alumna playwright of New Dramatists, contributing editor of *TheatreForum*, associate editor of *Contemporary Theatre Review* (Routledge/UK), Drama Editor of *Asymptote* literary journal, affiliate artist of New Georges, and founder of NoPassport theatre alliance and press. She holds an MFA from UCSD. Her website is www.caridadsvich.com

Second Son takes First Son's hand. They look at the water. Waves.

Music is heard midst the waves: sweet jazz from a long time past.

End of play

For they were motherless and fatherless,

And vanished to themselves.

They ate the grapes, and bit the leaves,

And chewed on the legs of insects.

They gorged themselves

with all manner of things:

Plants and brains and hard stones,

and fine claret

To soothe their tired tongues.

And when they were done feasting

They killed,

And not a goddamn did they give

About anything.

FIRST SON: ...You're older.

SECOND SON: I'm not.

FIRST SON: Are you sure?

SECOND SON: I'm the same. So are you.

Pause.

FIRST SON: Shall we go in?

SECOND SON: Now?

FIRST SON: The waves are coming up: beautiful, easy.

SECOND SON: ...Let's wait. We have time.

SECOND SON: He was sorry. He held me. I was in his arms for a long time.

FIRST SON: And then?

SECOND SON: He kissed me.

FIRST SON: A kiss is important.

SECOND SON: Yes. But it's not everything.

Pause.

FIRST SON: Do you think she loved us?

SECOND SON: Who?

FIRST SON: Tall woman with fierce eyes.

SECOND SON: I don't know who you mean.

FIRST SON: She held us both. Don't you remember?

SECOND SON: You held me. That's all I know.

FIRST SON: ...I'd like love in my life.

SECOND SON: Pure love?

FIRST SON: Stripped of everything.

SECOND SON: What would you do with it?

FIRST SON: Make something.

Pause.

SECOND SON: In olden times,

there were animals...

They came, and feasted on everything,

21.

Time passes. Waves. The boys are seen on the beach, un-marked.

They awaken slowly, and stare at the water.

SECOND SON: Was it like this?

FIRST SON: What?

SECOND SON: Swimming?

FIRST SON: Don't know.

SECOND SON: Don't you remember?

FIRST SON: I don't think I remember anything.

SECOND SON: Not even me?

FIRST SON: Of course I remember you. You're here.

SECOND SON: ...I remember a kiss.

FIRST SON: What kind?

SECOND SON: A brother's kiss. Very sweet.

FIRST SON: When was this?

SECOND SON: Not long ago.

FIRST SON: A brother?

SECOND SON: Yes. A dear brother of mine.

FIRST SON: ...What was he like?

SECOND SON: Taller. Older.

FIRST SON: Like me?

SECOND SON: He had tears in his eyes.

FIRST SON: How come?

20.

The Nurse is seen on beach's edge with radio in hand. He sees the boys' bodies.
Silence.

NURSE: If this I see is true...

what greater woe

now

for knowing

that what I have seen, and what I will see is forever marked

by love's selfish folly.

Infant joy of mine

wrecked joy - deliverance sweet...

I look up, and admit heaven.

For I am witness to all.

Listen now.

All will be found out:

the boys at sea, the elegant lady,

the man's cruelty...

For in my eyes, in my mouth, lives truth.

Y'hear?

The radio is heard: static.